Graphic Law and Drawn Justice

Graphic Law and Drawn Justice

A Legal Analysis

Edited by Giuseppe Martinico and
Gianpaolo Maria Ruotolo

ANTHEM PRESS

Anthem Press
An imprint of Wimbledon Publishing Company
www.anthempress.com

This edition first published in UK and USA 2025
by ANTHEM PRESS
75–76 Blackfriars Road, London SE1 8HA, UK
or PO Box 9779, London SW19 7ZG, UK
and
244 Madison Ave #116, New York, NY 10016, USA

British Library Cataloguing-in-Publication Data
A catalogue record for this book is available from the British Library.

Library of Congress Cataloging-in-Publication Data: 2024951841
A catalog record for this book has been requested.

ISBN-13: 978-1-83999-366-4 (Hbk)
ISBN-10: 1-83999-366-9 (Hbk)

This title is also available as an e-book.

To the superheroes of our multiverse.
Lelia, Angela, Francesco Maria and Clara Sofia: we love you 3000!
g&g

CONTENTS

List of Contributors ix

Chapter 1. Introduction 1
Giuseppe Martinico and Gianpaolo Maria Ruotolo

Chapter 2. *Daredevil*: Superheroes and Disability. Justice, Stigma and Law 5
Paolo Addis and Maria Giulia Bernardini

Chapter 3. Law and Justice in Comics: An Itinerary 17
Giuseppe Martinico

Chapter 4. From Pop Culture to Woke Culture? Law and Politics in the X-Men Saga 31
Luca Pietro Vanoni

Chapter 5. References to International Law in Harry Potter's Wizarding World 53
Angela Maria Gallo

Chapter 6. Doing International Law with Earbuds: Some Issues in Heavy Metal Music 67
Gianpaolo Maria Ruotolo

Chapter 7. The Multiple Characters of Francisco Ibáñez Talavera and the Law 97
Antoni Abat i Ninet

Chapter 8. 'Best Closer Beyond Rules' Between Legal Drama and Contemporary Public Ethics in Suits: Pop Culture Theory vs. Legal Culture? 115
Giovanna Tieghi

Chapter 9. Charlie Hebdo's Graphic Trial Reports (Cabu, Riss, Boucq) 129
Yasco Horsman

Chapter 10. Epilogue 141
Giuseppe Martinico and Gianpaolo Maria Ruotolo

Index 143

LIST OF CONTRIBUTORS

Antoni Abat i Ninet is Maria Zambrano Fellow at the Autonomous University of Barcelona, antoni.abat@uab.cat

Paolo Addis is Post Doc Fellow in Constitutional Law at Scuola Superiore Sant'Anna Pisa, paolo.addis@santannapisa.it

Maria Giulia Bernardini is Assistant Professor of Philosophy of Law at the University of Ferrara, brnmgl@unife.it

Giuseppe Martinico is Full Professor of Comparative Public Law at Scuola Superiore Sant'Anna Pisa, giuseppe.martinico@santannapisa.it

Angela Maria Gallo is a PhD candidate in International Law at Sapienza University in Rome, angelamaria.gallo@uniroma1.it

Yasco Horsman is Lecturer at the Leiden University Centre for the Arts in Society, y.horsman@hum.leidenuniv.nl

Gianpaolo Maria Ruotolo is Full Professor of International Law at the University of Foggia, gianpaolo.ruotolo@unifg.it

Giovanna Tieghi is a barrister and an Assistant Professor of Comparative Public Law at the University of Padua, giovanna.tieghi@unipd.it

Luca Pietro Vanoni is Associate Professor of Comparative Public Law at the University of Milan, luca.vanoni@gmail.com

Chapter 1

INTRODUCTION

Giuseppe Martinico and Gianpaolo Maria Ruotolo

This book explores how comics, animated series and pop music represent law, reflecting and shaping public perception. It adopts a comparative and international law approach, involving diverse scholars and going beyond Anglo-American culture to enrich the legal debate. This innovative collection fills a crucial gap in both legal and cultural studies.

While there is an established tradition in this field within Anglo-Saxon academic contexts,[1] in continental Europe, works like those included in this volume remain relatively rare.

This book is the product of a long journey that began before the pandemic and continued with virtual and in-person seminars that allowed us to gather a group of scholars interested in how the relationship between law and justice is represented in comics and other pop culture products.[2]

Over recent years, we have been organising an annual event that explores the intersection of law and pop culture. These events are primarily aimed at an academic audience but remain open to others. They bring together lawyers and non-lawyers – such as media sociologists and political philosophers – to examine the relationship between law and morality within various fictional worlds. The inaugural sessions featured Batman and Daredevil as focal points.

Inspired by the positive reception and media interest these events generated, the STALS research group (Sant'Anna Legal Studies)[3] hosted an

1 T. Giddens (ed.), *Graphic Justice: Intersections of Comics and Law* (Abingdon: Routledge, 2015).

2 R. K. Sherwin, *When Law Goes Pop: The Vanishing Line between Law and Popular Culture* (Chicago: University of Chicago Press, 2000). See also: A. Wagner and R. K. Sherwin, *Law, Culture and Visual Studies* (Berlin: Springer, 2014).

3 STALS (Sant'Anna Legal Studies) is a project made possible thanks to the financial support offered by Scuola Superiore Sant'Anna (Sant'Anna School of Advanced Studies), issued within the framework of the Sant'Anna School's internationalisation policy. It was founded by Paolo

online event titled *Law, Justice, and Pop Culture: An Interdisciplinary Dialogue.* This full-day event, which can be viewed on the STALS YouTube channel,[4] brought together diverse perspectives on the topic. Building on this momentum, we proposed to the Italian Society of Comparative and European Public Law (*Diritto pubblico comparato ed europeo*) that its annual conference, held in the Department of Law of the University of Foggia, should focus on the representation of legal traditions in pop culture. The call for papers, issued in Italian, attracted significant interest and culminated in a nearly 800-page volume edited by us, Aldo Ligustro and Rolando Tarchi.

Encouraged by the success of these initiatives, our STALS team – together with Paolo Addis and Luca Gori – decided to extend this project to high schools. We organised a series of lectures in Lucca, home to the renowned Lucca Comics & Games festival, Europe's largest comic and gaming convention. This initiative was carried out in partnership with the Centro Maria Eletta Martini, *Fondazione per la Coesione Sociale Onlus* and *Lucca Crea.* The first cycle included three sessions addressing complex legal issues, such as the interplay between law and revenge and the prohibition of torture in combating crime. Similar conferences were held in the South of Italy by the University of Foggia research group, such as those held in various editions of 'Festival del Nerd', a huge comic and gaming convention held in Foggia.

Trying to build on these initiatives, in 2024 we published the volume *The Law in Graphic Narratives: Legal Perspectives on Comics, Manga and Anime*, in De Gruyter's Law and Literature series.

That publication and its positive reception encouraged us to continue with this line of research, and this volume represents the ideal follow-up to that one. In this sense, we would like to thank Anthem Press for trusting us and believing in this project.

This volume attempts to bring together a group of authors from continental Europe to enrich the international debate on law and pop culture, for example, by bringing a different perspective on the role of law in the stories

---

Carrozza in 2008. Sant'Anna School of Advanced Studies is a public university institute – with special autonomy – working in the field of applied sciences. Sant'Anna School of Advanced Studies promotes the internationalisation of didactics and research with innovative paths in the fields of university education, scientific research and advanced training. Further info on the STALS programme can be found at the following URL: https://www.stals.santannapisa.it/ All our events are available at the following URL: https://www.youtube.com/@stalssantannalegalstudies8025

4 'Diritto, Giustizia e Cultura Pop. Un dialogo interdisciplinare', 18 November 2021 https://www.youtube.com/watch?v=ldxUcsHKXCI.

of famous Marvel and DC characters, but also by attempting to bring lesser-known stories from other contexts to the attention of the international public.

After this introduction, the book includes a chapter by Paolo Addis and Maria Giulia Bernardini on law and disability in Daredevil. Matt Murdock, Daredevil's alter ego, was blinded in a childhood accident involving radioactive chemicals. However, this loss of sight heightened his other senses to extraordinary levels, enabling him to navigate and combat crime with remarkable skill. For Addis and Bernardini, reflecting on Daredevil's adventures provides an opportunity to explore broader theoretical questions in law. Indeed, examining superheroes enables us to recognise the legal and political shortcomings created by their existence in these fictional universes. In so doing, they identify four key fault lines and offer an overarching interpretation of these tensions.

Martinico explains how analysing the portrayal of law in comics can provide valuable insights into key issues in legal theory and constitutional law. A central theme explored is the tension between law and morality, or law and religion, often conceptualised as a conflict between normative systems. These systems, while distinct, may overlap in certain aspects but rarely align completely. Law, morality and religion all function as normative frameworks, offering rules to guide individual behaviour. Martinico ultimately tackles two major questions: the issue of the insufficiency of law and the phenomenon of law as a source of discrimination.

Luca Pietro Vanoni's chapter delves into the interplay between law, politics and identity as portrayed in the X-Men saga within the Marvel Universe. He argues that the core of the X-Men story revolves around the conflict between *Homo sapiens* and *Homo superior*, reflecting broader themes of inclusion, exclusion and the challenges of embracing otherness. This explains why the X-Men have emerged as a powerful symbol of diversity, integration and resistance to discrimination.

In her chapter, Angela Maria Gallo examines the role of international law within the Wizarding World of Harry Potter. This fictional universe mirrors the real world in many respects; for instance, its depiction of State structures is fully fleshed out, with a clear representation of the separation of powers, particularly between the executive and judicial branches.

Similarly, the Wizarding World portrays an international community composed of States that collaborate to ensure global security for witches and wizards. This parallel to real-world international relations offers a fascinating perspective on how legal and political concepts are reimagined in fantasy literature.

Gianpaolo Maria Ruotolo explores the connections between comics and pop and rock music, with a focus on how themes related to international law are addressed in pop music. He then shifts his attention to heavy metal music, highlighting distinctive features that set it apart in its engagement with such issues. In so doing, he also explores the connection between comics and pop music and shows it is deeper than mere thematic overlaps.

Antoni Abat i Ninet analyses the genius of Francisco Ibáñez Talavera, defining him as one of the most important cultural figures of the last 50 years. In particular, Ibáñez's impact was even greater for the generation that witnessed Spain's democratic transformation and transition. This era saw the abolition of Francoist censorship and the rise of freedom of expression and the press.

Giovanna Tieghi offers a fresh account of Suits, a legal drama created by Aaron Korsh, suggesting that this TV show provides an evaluative lens through which the role of the lawyer is depicted. This portrayal has an immediate impact on the audience and shapes collective perceptions, but it also reflects the qualities that lawyers today must embody.

Finally, Yasco Horsman deals with Charlie Hebdo, the well-known French satirical weekly magazine and a seminal work in graphic journalism. By analysing both narrative style and graphic techniques employed by the artists, Horsman argues that the 'graphic trial report' from Charlie Hebdo offers a distinctive perspective on the dramatic dimensions of court proceedings, an aspect often overlooked in other visual and literary trial reports. Finally, in the epilogue, we aim to conclude this collective (and deliberately selective) reflection by offering some insights to further enrich our research agenda—one that is, for us, not only an intellectual pursuit but above all a passion, nurtured with the necessary rigor of legal studies.

Chapter 2

DAREDEVIL: SUPERHEROES AND DISABILITY. JUSTICE, STIGMA AND LAW

Paolo Addis and Maria Giulia Bernardini*

Preliminary Remarks

If we read the legal condition of persons with disabilities on the basis of the bio-psycho-social model as accepted by the ad hoc United Nations Convention on Rights of Persons with Disabilities of 2006 (UNCRPD), it is intuitive to try to trace the roots of disability in numerous cultural products. Indeed, although the bio-psycho-social model is not the only paradigm of disability currently widespread, on a legal level this model is nowadays accepted – expressly or not – within the legislative framework of many national systems, as well as the jurisprudential one, starting from the jurisprudence of the European Court of Human Rights (ECHR) and the Court of Justice of the European Union (CJEU). It is therefore a model aimed at providing a conceptual framework for understanding the 'disability phenomenon' on multiple levels, including the sociocultural and legal one.

In particular, starting from the idea that persons with disabilities – as stated in art. 1, paragraph II, UNCRPD – are those who 'have long-term physical, mental, intellectual or sensory impairments which in interaction with various barriers may hinder their full and effective participation in society on an equal basis with others', it is interesting to see how the mechanisms of inclusion and exclusion of persons with disabilities, which already originate at the level of cultural production, are represented, also in legal terms. To this end, it can certainly be useful to go beyond the (sometimes too narrow) boundaries of the specifically legal perimeter. Indeed, once it is understood that disability has a social root, to achieve an adequate understanding of the phenomenon

* All websites accessed on 20 November 2024.

and the dynamics that affect it, it is not only important, but even necessary to refer to the various 'Laws & [...]'. Referencing Law & Movies is useful for legal scholars, because cinema is a lens which often reveals the social and cultural perception of certain legal institutions or of the justice system as a whole.

References to the complex relationship between disability and cinema are countless: the public display of 'abnormality' has constituted a sort of *continuum*, at least from the sixteenth century to today. From this point of view, limiting our analysis to the American cinematographic context, it is easy to think of the well-known *Freaks*, by Tod Browning (1932), or *The Elephant Man* by David Lynch (1980); in more recent times, it is perhaps *The Shape of Water*, by Guillermo Del Toro (2018), that has drawn attention to disability as a deviation from the norm, from which society must, *à la Foucault*, defend itself.

From a legal perspective, it is certainly interesting to pay attention to the way in which the law has historically dealt with such an anomalous and dangerous object as disability. Legal historical investigations reveal how, between the mid-nineteenth and mid-twentieth centuries, one of the main forms of 'management' of disability was constituted, in the United States, by the Ugly Laws; these were measures often approved and applied by local authorities, with the aim of preventing the 'public peace' from being disturbed by what – due to its 'monstrosity' – was better hidden from view.

Even outside of this strand, the examples are truly innumerable: the movie *One Flew Over the Cuckoo's Nest*, by Miloš Forman (1976), takes up many themes already covered by Erving Goffman 15 years earlier[1] and at the end of the '80s, autism and cultural barriers are the subject of the film *Rain Man* (1988). In times much closer to our own, during the 2022 Oscar Awards Ceremony, *CODA*, which tells a story featuring persons with disabilities as protagonists, was awarded Best Film.[2]

Such complexity – which implies a variety of themes, approaches and methods of analysis – therefore requires a delimitation of the field. In this chapter, we will focus on the figure of a superhero, in whose adventures disability often appears:[3] the reflections developed here start from the character

1 E. Goffman, *Asylums: Essays on the Condition of the Social Situation of Mental Patients and Other Inmates* (New York: Anchor Books, 1961).

2 'CODA' is an acronym that stands for child of deaf adult(s), used to specifically refer to a hearing person who has a deaf parent or parents. See also V. S. Hosley, *Film Starring Actors with Disabilities Makes Oscars History*, 29 March 2022, available at https://www.disabilityscoop.com/2022/03/29/film-starring-actors-with-disabilities-makes-oscars-history/29777/.

3 About disability in the Marvel Universe, see J. Grue, 'Ablenationalists Assemble! On Disability in the Marvel Cinematic Universe', *Journal of Literary and Cultural Disability Studies*, 15, no. 1 (2021): 1–17. On the relationship between law, justice and religion in Daredevil, see L. J. A. Brown,

of Daredevil and from the representation given to him in cinema[4] and in TV shows, rather than in Marvel comics. Our starting point is the story of Matthew Murdock, who became blind due to an accident with a radioactive substance that occurred as a teenager and who, as an adult, divides his time between the courtrooms, being a lawyer by day and a superhero who fights the criminals he couldn't nail in the courtroom by night. Recalling the adventures of Daredevil will also allow us to question ourselves on more general theoretical legal issues: dealing with superheroes allows us to understand the legal and political shortcomings which make the presence of a superhero necessary. We will try to identify four possible fault lines and give a summary reading of them; the first of them concerns the 'classic' tension between law and justice, sometimes resulting in a decisive and radical distance.

Law *and* Justice or Law *against* Justice?

The often-conflicting relationship between law and justice is one of the most important subjects of study in legal philosophy, where it is examined in relation to multiple aspects, among which the attention to the configuration of the 'justice system' as a whole, as well as the tension between legality and justice, is particularly notable.[5] In relation to this last aspect, one need only think of the Greek myth concerning Sophocles' Antigone, who decides to bury the body of her brother Polynices against the will of the King of Thebes, Creon, who had forbidden it with a decree, and for this, she is condemned to imprisonment.[6] Furthermore, the tension between legality and justice emerges strongly in totalitarian experiences, when the problem of the distance between the law

'Daredevil: Vigilantes, Villains, the Law, and Morality', in *The Law in Graphic Narratives. Legal Perspectives on Comics, Manga and Anime*, eds. G. Martinico and G. M Ruotolo (Berlin: De Gruyter, 2024): 11–32, and A. Negri, 'Divine or Human Justice? Law and Religion in Daredevil Comics', in *The Law in Graphic Narratives. Legal Perspectives on Comics, Manga and Anime*, eds. G. Martinico and G. M Ruotolo (Berlin: De Gruyter, 2024): 33–48.

4 Especially in the movie *Daredevil* directed by M. S. Johnson (2003).

5 Significant in this regard are Alf Ross' notable considerations: 'The idea of law is generally taken to mean justice, which leads to questions concerning the content and basis of the principle of justice; concerning the relation between justice and positive law; the role of the principle of justice as regards legislation, the application of law, and so on'. Cf. A. Ross, 'The Problems of Legal Philosophy', in *On Law and Justice*, eds. J. v. H. Holtermann and U. Bindreiter (Oxford, 2019; online ed, Oxford Academic, 23 January 2020): 7–39. https://doi.org/10.1093/oso/9780198716105.003.0001.

6 For an introduction to the topic, see T. Burns, 'Sophocles' Antigone and the History of the Concept of Natural Law', *Political Studies*, 50, no. 3 (2002): 545–557. https://doi.org/10.1111/1467-9248.00384.

produced by the 'unjust' – but lawful – power and justice reveals itself in all its dramatic intensity. If, according to the ethical legalism embraced at the time, 'the law is the law' and as such must be obeyed, the 'intolerably unjust'[7] content revealed by totalitarian laws prompts questions about the legal value to be attributed to unjust law and, consequently, its obligatory nature, leading to a lively doctrinal debate where often highly heterogeneous responses have been provided.

The advent of constitutional States has facilitated the response: in addition to formal constraints, there are also substantive limits that laws must adhere to within different legal systems.[8] Yet, even this response does not fully address the relationship between law (understood as legality) and justice: numerous doubts remain, which continue to be raised, in a sort of 'eternal return of the same'. We might ask, for example: are these limits to law, including the substantive ones, sufficient enough to ensure justice? Is it possible to achieve a perfect coincidence between legality and justice? What is the ideal of justice to strive for? Does it make sense to think of justice in abstract terms? Where does the power of those who administer justice (i.e. the judges) come from? Does their action always achieve the objective set by the legal system?

The answer to the last question suggested by Daredevil is negative, as Matthew Murdock/Daredevil constantly finds himself at the centre of events where his presence is considered necessary, as an expression of a kind of justice different from the one guaranteed by the law.

This idea of justice 'beyond' the law, embodied by a superhero who acts precisely to achieve 'real justice', links Daredevil to other superheroes. Nonetheless, the motivations behind the actions carried out by them can be quite varied, due to the narrative choice regarding the initial decision that sealed their fate. For example, another famous superhero, Bruce Wayne/Batman, decided to fight crime not out of an abstract desire for justice, but to avenge his parents who were killed during a robbery attempt.[9]

This difference in motivations is reflected in the depiction of Daredevil himself, who is a tormented superhero, perhaps because he is more 'human' and 'real'. Maybe this unease could be attributed to a religious aspect (which

---

7 G. Radbruch, 'Gesetzliches Unrecht und übergesetzliches Recht', *Süddeutsche Juristen-Zeitung*, 1, no. 5 (1946): 105–108.

8 Luigi Ferrajoli has long addressed the requirement of the formal and substantive validity of the law: see L. Ferrajoli, *La democrazia attraverso i diritti. Il costituzionalismo garantista come modello teorico e come progetto politico* (Roma-Bari: Laterza, 2013).

9 On this point, see T. Giddens, 'Natural Law and Vengeance: Jurisprudence on the Streets of Gotham', *International Journal for the Semiotics of Law*, 28 (2015): 765–785 and, in this book, Giuseppe Martinico's essay.

is generally not present in the biographies of superheroes) that emerges especially in two scenes from the 2003 film, which seem particularly relevant for understanding the ethical dimension of the character. The first is the opening scene of the film: Daredevil, the hero, injured, descends into the nave of a large Catholic Church. Later, in the course of the film, we witness his confession, during which the priest emphasises how justice cannot in any way be reduced to revenge.

While of considerable interest, the religious dimension of justice cannot be explored further here: the reference to the law requires us to focus on the possible – and indeed, frequent – tension between legality and justice. In the events featuring Daredevil as the protagonist, the legal system is concerned with solving the case and *always finding an answer*, regardless of the methods used and whether the answer is the right one: a culprit must be found in any case.

Such dynamics are not unfamiliar to the jurists. One might think of the difference between the historical truth and the procedural one: in almost every legal system, practical reasons of judicial economy have led to the point where a decision must be made based on the available evidence, even if all the necessary elements are not present. Therefore, it is possible that the 'true' truth is never fully revealed, but only the 'plausible', that is, a form of 'approximate' truth.[10]

The image of Daredevil as a hero emerges precisely in relation to this aspect: he opposes the legal order because he is concerned with justice and truth. This positioning of the superhero leads us to question the necessary correlation between law and justice and suggests the opportunity of critically considering the relationship between evil and illegality. In other words, illegal actions are not necessarily 'evil', but they may lead to the realisation of 'true' justice.

From this perspective, the superhero becomes an *a-legal phenomenon* and reveals the complexity of the relationship between law and justice by operating *outside the law*, that is, in the absence of law or, at best, where the law is highly indeterminate. In this way, the superhero becomes the law itself, the law of justice, which clearly has nothing to do with divine justice or natural law. Indeed, in limiting the use of violence against his opponent, Daredevil affirms: 'I detest what he does [...], what he is. But I'm not God. I'm not the Law. And I'm not a murderer'.

---

10 *Ex multis*, on this topic cf. M. Taruffo, *La semplice verità. Il giudice e la ricostruzione dei fatti* (Roma-Bari: Laterza, 2009).

On closer inspection, the tension between law and justice emerges even before Daredevil's choice to act against the legal system or in its place: it can be traced back to his very existence and, in particular, to his condition of disability. Daredevil's blindness leads us to consider him as the embodiment of justice, which is typically represented as blind, that is, devoid of sight.[11]

Furthermore, this very specificity prompts questions about the particular relationship between persons with disabilities and access to justice, a human right that is often characterised by a considerable rate of ineffectiveness. This is an aspect that we cannot go into here, but which has been the subject of specific analyses, and which suggests the great conceptual and value stratification that – albeit often unconsciously – drives us to (re)interpret the complex relationship between justice and disability.[12]

On a more general level, the relationship between Daredevil, law and justice appears ambivalent, marked by various tensions and contradictions. Matt Murdock works in court as a lawyer, and as such, he adheres to the forms and rituals that govern that space (primarily expressed in the rules of due process[13]). Nevertheless, a challenge to the law (or at least to a specific conception) is always present, and it seems to emerge in relation to several aspects. Indeed, Daredevil/Murdock carries out his challenges to the justice system both from the outside and from within. As a superhero, Daredevil acts outside the courts, radically denouncing the partiality of the justice system. He really 'delivers justice' when he dons the superhero guise, although this does not prevent him from being conflicted by multiple ethical doubts.

There is also a challenge to the justice system that moves in the opposite direction, that is, from within. As a lawyer, Matt Murdock opposes, for example, the use of delaying tactics and the exploitation of people, leaning

11 In this regard, we refer to the insightful analysis of A. Prosperi, *Giustizia bendata. Percorsi storici di un'immagine* (Torino: Einaudi, 2008) and J. Resnik and D. Curtis, *Representing Justice: Invention, Controversy, and Rights in City-States and Democratic Courtrooms* (New Haven: Yale University Press, 2011). It should be noted that although the depiction of blindfolded justice is the most widespread, it is nevertheless not the only one.

12 Cfr. D. Dorfman, 'The Blind Justice Paradox: Judges with Visual Impairments and the Disability Metaphor', *Cambridge Journal of International and Comparative Law*, 5, no. 2 (2016): 272–305. In recent times, the Court of Justice of the European Union has also considered the issue: cf. CGUE, C-824/19, *Komisia za zashtita ot diskriminatsia*, 21 October 2021, commented by P. Addis, 'Una persona con disabilità può far parte di una giuria? Note a partire dal caso Komisia za zashtita ot diskriminatsiadella Corte di giustizia', *DPCEonline*, 1 (2022): 429–436.

13 See L. M. Rosen, 'The Lawyer as Superhero: How Marvel Comics' Daredevil Depicts the American Court System and Legal Practice', *Capital University Law Review*, 47 (2019): 379.

in this case towards the deontological model of the 'good lawyer'.[14] In fact, as a lawyer, Matt Murdock uses abilities that, upon closer inspection, are extraordinary, like the ability to hear the heartbeat of witnesses on the stand to determine if they are lying. In this way, he tries to remain honest and ethically consistent within a system where the connection to power and the vast availability of money encourage episodes of corruption. When related to the previous one, this aspect brings to the fore the relevance of one of the main issues in legal ethics, concerning the relationship between an individual's ethical character and their professional competence: can a good person also be a (good) lawyer?[15]

Finally, and even more radically, Daredevil challenges the rationality of the law from a context – the courtroom – where rationality is traditionally one of the cornerstone elements of the legal phenomenon, as it serves to present the law as the only possible world. Through his actions, the superhero demonstrates that a critique of the existing legal order can be appropriate (and even necessary). As a lawyer, Matt Murdock is certainly required to use rationality, remaining faithful to the teachings of his father, a boxer who was killed by organised crime for refusing to rig a match. It was his father who taught him to use his mind rather than force and violence (and the law itself has the primary function of prohibiting the unjustified use of force). However, Murdock also finds himself dealing with a strong emotional component, which he displays at night by using that very force that he seems to keep under control during the daytime, in the realm of visibility. This is merely an appearance: the resort to force does not abandon him even during the day, sometimes even putting his clients' interests at risk when – ethically speaking – his secret superhero identity intertwines with his professional career.

This aspect, in turn, allows us to glimpse another way in which Matt Murdock/Daredevil challenges the law or, more precisely, its 'legal architecture', which rests on the separation of roles and powers. Upon closer inspection, our superhero is a lawyer by day but a judge by night. One might wonder whether this blending of roles, which from a legal perspective appears to be a clear regression from the principles governing the liberal state of law, can truly be considered an expression of justice. What becomes of the impartiality

---

14 In legal ethics, the references regarding the figure of the 'good lawyer' are numerous, starting from the famous D. Luban (ed.), *The Good Lawyer: Lawyers' Roles and Lawyers' Ethics* (Totowa: Rowman & Allanheld, 1983).

15 See, e.g., D. Thunder, 'Can a Good Person be a Lawyer', *Notre Dame Journal of Law, Ethics & Public Policy*, 20, no. 1 (2006): 313–334; A. Woolley and W. Bradley Wendel, 'Legal Ethics and Moral Character', *Georgetown Journal of Legal Ethics*, 23 (2010): 1065; D. Luban, 'How Must a Lawyer Be? A Response to Woolley and Wendel', *Georgetown Journal of Legal Ethics*, 23 (2010): 1101.

of the judge, which is widely regarded as one of the foundations of the rule of law?

'What's up, freak?': Daredevil's Disability

A second interesting profile concerns the impairment and disability of Matt Murdock/Daredevil.[16]

Preliminarily, it has been underlined that the *actual* Daredevil has a predecessor and namesake, which dates to an era of American comics prior to the birth of Marvel, during the 1940s. It was then, in fact, that the first Daredevil – who in his ordinary life was called Barth Hill and not Matt Murdock – was invented, and who was not blind, but mute. This change does not seem secondary: the passage from one type of impairment to another can be interpreted as an expression of a normative judgement towards different disabilities. Indeed, historically, blindness seems to have been more socially accepted than other types of disability. *Being blind* does not disturb the order as happens, for example, in the case of the complex world of mental disability. From this perspective, blindness can therefore be a hero's disability: it creates disorientation, but at the same time, this choice is acceptable from the point of view of current cultural canons.

Seeing, then, tells us something about *recognition* and *inclusion*. As pointed out, *invisibility* constitutes an acute form of social discrimination, characterised by structural exclusion and based on socially widespread stereotypes. From this point of view, we can say that making blindness one of the characteristics of the superhero allows us to make this existential aspect notable and, therefore, to make Matt Murdock/Daredevil a socially included human being. If this choice is understandable, it also creates a problem; it could be argued that such a choice creates hierarchies between the various disabilities. The question does not appear far-fetched: the movement for the civil rights of persons with disabilities has long prioritised physical disabilities over mental ones. It could therefore be hypothesised that the Daredevil world constitutes a specific case of a more widespread problem of a structural nature.

Again, with specific reference to the type of impairment from which Daredevil's disability arises, other interesting aspects emerge.

---

16 It is worth pointing out that Daredevil is not the only superhero with a disability, nor the last one in order of appearance; e.g., Doctor Xavier of *X-Men* is quadriplegic. In 2010, a superhero with Down syndrome, *Metaphase*, made his debut on Kickstarter; currently, *Metaphase* is published in the United States by Alterna Comics.

Daredevil is a *metropolitan superhero*, and his space of action is physically well reconstructed and contextualised: the city in which he acts is New York and the Hell's Kitchen is his neighbourhood.[17] Living in urban space cannot be taken for granted: although the culture of accessibility of physical spaces has experienced a notable expansion starting from the years in which Stan Lee created the current version of Daredevil, with the approval, even in the United States of America, of substantial State and federal regulations relating to the removal of architectural barriers.[18]

It is significant how, in the *Daredevil* 2003 movie, the dangerousness of the urban environment is highlighted in numerous scenes: New York City is full of obstacles and risks, even for persons without disabilities. From this point of view, Daredevil's ability to adequately use the surrounding urban space, fighting with great effectiveness against enemies without disabilities even in places such as a playground or a subway, contributes to the consolidation of a superhero image. His ability to emerge victorious fundamentally serves to highlight his *extraordinary nature*. In the eyes of those who deal with disability law and disability studies, however, it also serves to draw attention to the theme of politics and ethics relating to spaces built and inhabited by human beings, as well as their inclusiveness.[19]

What Space for a 'Super-subjectivity' with Disability?

Through this path, we are led to question the dynamics of the inclusion of people with disabilities, raising a series of even more radical questions than those that have emerged so far: is it truly the case that by linking disability to heroism, we promote the 'redemption' of the disabled subject, its liberation from failure and inevitable misfortune? What image of disability is represented through a superhero? How is disability 'constructed', and in what way is its visibility promoted? Must inclusion and visibility of persons with disabilities necessarily go through the exaltation of heroic deeds? Doesn't this strategy favour rather a separation between those people with disabilities who are able, *despite the misfortune that has befallen them*,[20] to be 'special' and 'super'

17 About Hell's Kitchen as a Hobbesian political space, see A. P. Spanakos, 'Hell's Kitchen's Prolonged Crisis and Would-be Sovereign: Daredevil, Hobbes, and Schmitt', *PS: Political Science and Politics*, 47, no. 1 (2014): 94–97.

18 See B. Williamson, *Accessible America: A History of Disability and Design* (New York: New York University Press, 2019).

19 M. Kingwell, *The Ethics of Architecture* (Oxford: Oxford University Press, 2021).

20 The idea of disability as an inexorable individual misfortune forms the basis of the famous 'medical model' of disability, the straw man developed within Disability Studies, which we invoke here with a clear critical intent.

and those who remain unable to perform such deeds, and for this reason, end up facing a kind of 'double failure'?[21] In short, does not this strategy of recognition reproduce the 'medical model' that views disability necessarily as a tragedy and a lack of the characteristics considered necessary to be regarded as typically human?

These questions would require detailed answers, which we cannot articulate in this context. For now, we limit ourselves to observing how in Daredevil one of the problems was precisely related to understanding the most correct way to narrate and represent blindness.

Normally, blindness is considered a lack of a sense that leads to the inability to function in the 'typically human' way and to conform to role expectations. Thus, this lack signals a more general incompatibility with society as a whole. Yet, even in the 1980s, the comic that preceded the TV series and the film did not use the language of lack, although it contained 'clues' suggesting that the cultural legacy was still one that saw disability as 'something' that negatively impacts one's humanity.[22] The underlying cultural paradigm was thus the 'medical' one, and it could hardly have been otherwise, since it was only in 1981 that the Disability Studies field theorised the 'social model' of disability, which would lead to a radical shift in approach towards disability itself.[23]

Upon closer inspection, another aspect proves that the character of Daredevil can be attributed to the 'medical model' of disability. His extraordinary abilities serve as compensation for a loss resulting from performing a good deed, within a framework that could be described as compensatory justice. While the narrative intent is clear – and not in question here – it is worth asking again whether this technique promotes the recognition of equal dignity for the subjectivity of people with disabilities, or rather adheres to a cultural model in which disability is viewed as an inexorable misfortune that must be compensated, or in some way entitled to a form of compensation.

On the other hand, this recovery of the individual's functional limitation also brings to the surface the theme of vulnerability, which appears in Daredevil in various forms: the social vulnerability of Hell's Kitchen (i.e. the

21 On one hand, they do not conform to the norms of the able-bodied, and on the other, neither do they fit the model of a person with a disability who redeems themselves from the personal tragedy they have endured.

22 In this regard, one can think of the scene where Matt Murdock explains that he tried to excel in school to prove that he could be human despite his disability.

23 For this model, disability is a form of oppression (i.e. systemic discrimination) imposed on those with an impairment: see P. Abberley, 'The Concept of Oppression and the Development of a Social Theory of Disability', *Disability & Society*, 2, no. 1 (1987): 5–19.

real context of reference), and above all, the emotional and bodily vulnerability of Matt Murdock/Daredevil.

In the past, this aspect has sometimes led to viewing Daredevil as a 'minor' hero, in a sense, precisely because he is visibly vulnerable. On the contrary, nowadays the 'vulnerability turn'[24] allows us to better understand the universality of the concept of limits and the impossibility of considering it a valid reason to establish hierarchies between lives, or to make distinctions between a full humanity and a diminished one. Some limits, like those which can emerge in the case of disability, do not arise from an existential specificity but are rather the product of a socio-institutional setup that was created without accounting for certain subjects, who were removed from the symbolic and cultural space before even being confined to specific physical spaces precisely because of that specificity.

Final Remarks: Daredevil and the US Approach to the Rights of Persons with Disabilities

Finally, Daredevil stories allow us to illustrate some of the ways in which US law regulates the legal condition of persons with disabilities. First, it is necessary to keep in mind a starting circumstance: Daredevil is a character created by Stan Lee in 1964. On the one hand, his paternity can provide a possible causal explanation of the strong individualistic connotation of the character, since Stan Lee was a self-made man, born in poor conditions, who began working as a teenager and created a whole imaginary universe loved by millions of people.[25] On the other hand, it should be noted that 1964 is the year in which President Lyndon B. Johnson signed the Civil Rights Act. It was a moment of historical and legal transition: in the same period, the North American Disability Rights Movement was born. Anyway, as already said, Daredevil took the first steps in an era in which the medical model of disability was mainstream: it was the individual who had to face his own disability, alone.

Now, despite the decline of the medical model, individualism, as is known, is strongly present in American legal and political culture. As it has been argued,[26] in the disability legal framework, anti-discrimination law is often

24 Cfr. L. Burgogue-Larsen (ed.), *La vulnérabilité saisies par les judges en Europe* (Paris: Pedone, 2014).

25 About Stan Lee's life, see A. Riesman, *True Believer: The Rise and Fall of Stan Lee* (New York: Crown, 2022).

26 S. R. Bagenstos, *Law and the Contradictions of the Disability Rights Movement* (New Haven: Yale University Press, 2009): 'Unlike a presentation of disability rights laws as the logical next step in the increasingly fragile expansion of civil rights protections, the presentation of disability rights

presented as essential to preserving the self-determination, autonomy and independence of the persons with disabilities. Daredevil, from the European side of the Atlantic, embodies well what appears to be one of the limits of US policies for the inclusion of persons with disabilities. From such a perspective, a possible enrichment for the US legal system, as it has been underlined, could come from the ratification of the UN Convention on the Rights of Persons with Disabilities.[27]

---

laws as a means of achieving independence resonated strongly with the ascendant conservative ethic of individualism, self-reliance, and fiscal restraint': 29.

27 A. S. Kanter, 'Let's Try Again: Why the United States Should Ratify the United Nations Convention on the Rights of People with Disabilities', *Touro Law Review*, 35, no. 1 (2019): 301–343.

Chapter 3

LAW AND JUSTICE IN COMICS: AN ITINERARY

Giuseppe Martinico*

Why Study Law in Comics?

In this chapter, I will try to explain why the analysis of the representation of law provided by comics can be very useful in shedding light on some major themes of legal theory and constitutional law. In a seminal piece, Asimow[1] emphasised the potential of pop culture when teaching law courses:

> First, consider pop culture as a mirror. The media of popular culture (in the narrow sense) illuminate what many people actually believe. These works reflect the dominant ideologies of society [...] Of course, pop culture never accurately reflects the world it depicts, for these are works of fiction, produced to entertain mass audiences and to make a profit [...] Second, consider pop culture as a lamp. People learn a great deal in the process of consuming pop culture. Popular culture (in the narrow sense) powerfully constructs what people believe (popular culture in the broad sense).[2]

There are certainly advantages and disadvantages to this exercise that also apply to the use of comics. On the one hand, students will certainly be aided in their understanding of legal dynamics by the use of comic book stories and characters. The use of comics will also reduce the existing gap in knowledge

---

* All websites accessed on 30 August 2024.

1 M. Asimow, 'The Mirror and the Lamp', *Journal of Legal Education* 68, no. 1 (2018): 115–121. More in general on teaching with comics see: R. Aman and L. Wallner (eds.), *Teaching with Comics: Empirical, Analytical, and Professional Experiences* (Berlin: Springer, 2022).

2 Asimow (see note 1): 116–117.

between professors and students,[3] in the sense that students will be able to start from a knowledge of the stories that will facilitate interaction. On the other hand, the vision that comics offer of law is certainly simplified or, rather, presents the same clichés that ordinary people have of law. As a law professor, I have to say that my students have generally always been more fascinated by outlaws than by the guardians of legality. Make no mistake, though, here the notion of outlaw does not necessarily include only villains, but also many of what we would call superheroes. This is also explained by the fact that the world in which these actors operate is often based on corrupt power dynamics. In this chapter, I will try to show the usefulness of comics-based legal research in investigating the pathological side of law, with particular reference to two phenomena: the insufficiency of law in the fight for justice and the use of laws as instruments for creating discrimination.[4] These are obviously only two examples among many possible ones. In this sense, the chapter makes no claim to exhaustiveness.

The relationship between justice and law is a classic in legal and political theory and has offered many insights to law and humanities studies, starting with the well-known events of Antigone, which 'is a tragedy about law and its inherent conflicts'.[5] In Sophocles' tragedy, a woman defied the laws of the city of Thebes (and of political power) to bury her brother, as was right according to ancient divine laws:

> Your edict, King, was strong,
> But all your strength is weakness itself against
> The immortal unrecorded laws of God.
> They are not merely now: they were, and shall be,
> Operative for ever, beyond man utterly.
> I knew I must die, even without your decree: I am only mortal. And if I must die

---

3 'Normally, the teacher is the expert, and the students passively absorb the teacher's knowledge. But in a course based on the vehicles of popular culture, the students share expertise with the instructor. All the students in the room are already experts in interpreting pop culture. They know the language of film and television. They have been practicing that language since before they learned to talk, much less read. Every student has seen hundreds of movies and thousands of television shows. In many cases, the students have consumed more popular culture than the instructor has', Asimow (see note 1): 115.

4 J. Daily, 'Mutants and Anti-Discrimination Laws, Part One', 19 November 2010, https://lawandthemultiverse.com/2010/11/19/mutants-and-anti-discrimination-laws-one/ and J. Daily, 'Mutants and Anti-Discrimination Laws, Part Two', 19 November 2010, https://lawandthemultiverse.com/2010/11/19/mutants-and-anti-discrimination-laws-two/.

5 T. Staehler, 'Antigone and the Nature of Law', in *Law and Philosophy, Current Legal Issues*, eds. M. Freeman and R. Harrison (Oxford: Oxford University Press, 2007): 137–156.

Now, before it is my time to die,
Surely this is no hardship: can anyone Living, as I live, with evil all about me,
Think Death less than a friend? This death of mine
Is of no importance; but if I had left my brother
Lying in death unburied, I should have suffered. Now I do not. You smile at me. Ah Creon,
Think me a fool, if you like; but it may well be
That a fool convicts me of folly.[6]

This conflict between law and morality or between law and religion is often described as a conflict between normative systems, which almost never totally coincide, although they can sometimes present forms of overlap. Law, morality and religion are all normative systems that express themselves in norms designed to guide the conduct of individuals. This also anticipates the problem that will be addressed in the second part of the chapter: the injustice of the law. This issue is familiar to scholars of authoritarian and totalitarian systems, in which law does not act as a barrier to injustice, but as an instrument used by political power to fulfil the political designs of the ruling elite.

The common thread of both parts of the chapter is that of legal injustice, which confirms the insufficiency of law and explains the phenomenon of law as a source of discrimination.

The Insufficiency of the Law: The Case of Batman

Comic books provide a unique lens on the portrayal of the legal and political spheres and the world of Batman fiction is no exception. In the chaotic realm of Gotham, law is far from being an instrument of justice due to the pervasive corruption that extends even to the police force. This is vividly illustrated in *Batman: Year One*, where the early career of Lieutenant Gordon reveals his struggle in a city where the mayor and police commissioner use officers as hired assassins. This backdrop leads Gordon to reassess Batman: 'He's a criminal. I'm a cop. It's that simple. But – but I'm a cop in a city where the mayor and the commissioner of police use cops as hired killers'.[7]

6 Sophocles, *Antigone*, 442 BC, English translation by D. Fitts and R. Fitzgerald (San Diego: Harcourt, Brace and Co., 1939). Full text in English also available at: https://mthoyibi.wordpress.com/wp-content/uploads/2011/05/antigone_2.pdf.

7 *Batman: Year One, Batman* by Frank Miller, 1987.

By the time of *Batman: Year Two*,[8] Commissioner Gordon describes the relationship between the Gotham police and Batman as cooperative, even though Batman insists on working alone. Later, in *The Dark Knight Returns*,[9] a veteran Gordon admits he has 'bent and sometimes broken'[10] the rules to collaborate with Batman. This complex relationship underscores the allure Batman holds for legal scholars. He operates outside the law, challenging the Weberian ideal of the State monopoly of the legitimate use of physical force,[11] yet his actions are undeniably driven by a sense of justice.

In *The Long Halloween*,[12] this dynamic is captured in a scene where Gordon and Dent, still serving as Gotham City's district attorney, wait for Batman on one of Gotham's iconic rooftops before taking action. As Thomas Giddens observes, this scene exemplifies a true triumvirate: Gordon (representing the police) and Dent (the legal system) depend on Batman (the symbol of justice) to ensure their actions are guided by a genuine desire for justice.[13]

However, to those who adhere strictly to the letter of the law, Batman appears not so different from the criminals he pursues. The theme of the 'closeness' between Batman and the Joker has persisted over the years. Aside from Batman's famous 'don't kill' rule (which was not always a part of his early stories), the two characters share more similarities than one might expect, as the Joker himself highlights in *The Killing Joke*.[14] In a scene from the animation movie[15] (which differs somewhat from Alan Moore's comic), after kidnapping and torturing Gordon, the Joker and his freaks confront him with a series of questions:

> '*Freaks:* What should be done with someone who has no regard for the law?'
> Someone who treats people like meat?
> 'A man who has no problem brutalizing his fellow man to get his way?'
> 'What would you do to a man who breaks the laws you are sworn to uphold?'
> 'A monster who ignores everything you stand for?' [...]
> *Gordon:* 'If it were up to me, I'd throw the book at him'. [...]
> *Joker:* 'Truth is, Commissioner, the man on trial here you consider your friend'.[16]

---

8 *Batman: Year Two* by Mike W. Barr, 1987.

9 *Batman: The Dark Knight Returns* by Frank Miller, 1986.

10 *Batman: The Dark Knight Returns* by Frank Miller, 1986.

11 M. Weber, 'Politics as a Vocation', in *From Max Weber: Essays in Sociology*, eds. H. H. Gerth and C. Wright Mills (Oxford: Oxford University Press, 1958): 77128.

12 *Batman: The Long Halloween* by Jeph Loeb, 1996–1997.

13 T. Giddens, 'Natural Law and Vengeance. International Journal for the Semiotics of Law', *Revue internationale de Semiotigue juridique* 28, no. 4 (2015): 765–785, 766.

14 *Batman: The Killing Joke* by Alan Moore, 1988.

15 *Batman: The Killing Joke*, the film directed by Sam Liu, 2016.

16 *Batman: The Killing Joke*, the film directed by Sam Liu, 2016.

The Joker's intention was precisely to demonstrate how Batman also represents a subject to be sentenced with the maximum sentence, and Batman, in fact, frequently demonstrates that he puts his justice before the law, which seems, at times, to be confused with the desire for revenge.

However, for Batman, justice goes beyond revenge as can be inferred from *Batman: Year Two*, in which the murderer of Bruce Wayne's parents, Joe Chill, appears on the scene. To fight Gotham's old vigilante, the Reaper, Batman agrees to ally himself with his parents' murderer. The Reaper is another key figure in understanding the role of law in Batman's world. The Reaper is back on the scene in Gotham because he considers Batman weak because of his 'code' ('don't kill'). Batman and the Reaper have something in common: the instrumental use of fear, just think of the 'battle cry' of the latter ('Fear [...] the Reaper'[17]). However, there are two crucial differences between these two characters: the Reaper has no faith in the law and, above all, he does not hesitate to take the lives of criminals. It is precisely the power to decide the lives of criminals that makes the Reaper a fully-fledged villain in the eyes of Batman and Gordon.

Nevertheless, Batman sometimes falters and risks violating his code of honour. This is the case, for example, in *Batman: Hush*, in which Commissioner Gordon intervenes to prevent the killing of the Joker, recalling the great difference between Batman and the supervillains he prosecutes:

> You and I have seen more than our fair share of tragedies and thirsted for revenge. If Batman wanted to be a killer, he could have started long ago. But, it's a line. On one side we believe in the law. On the other [...] sometimes, the law fails us. Maybe that's why I've understood you [...] allowed you to help protect this city.
>
> Batman, if you cross that line – if you kill The Joker tonight – I will lead the hunt to bring you to justice. In the eyes of the law [...] in my eyes you'll be no different from him.[18]

The line that then distinguishes Batman from the thugs in Gordon's eyes is precisely the maintenance of the 'do not kill' rule. However, this is not enough to bring Batman back into the sphere of legality. After all, the hooded detective describes himself as a criminal in an epic scene in *Batman: The Dark Knight Returns*, in which he and Superman fight bitterly. In the dialogue between the

17 *Batman: Year Two* by Mike W. Barr, 1987.
18 *Batman: Hush* by Jeph Loeb, 2003.

two heroes, Superman accuses Batman of behaving like a criminal, provoking the Caped Crusader's piqued response:

> '*Clark Kent:* "Why do you always have to be like this? You played right into their hands last time, when the parents groups and subcommittees came after us, you're the one they pointed to. You act like a criminal".
> *Bruce Wayne:* "We are criminals, Clark. We always have been. You're still one too. Only difference is you have a boss"'.[19]

However, Batman must be contextualised: he is the product of a system that fails to deliver justice, in a world of broken rules where public power has modest resources. This is also why, it has been suggested by Thomas Giddens, Batman operates as 'an emanation of natural law [...] thus demonstrating that to which the system should be aspiring, what the system should be'.[20]

Against this background, scholars have discussed the possibility of seeing in Batman the emanation of constituent power. Constituent power is a concept that comes from European political and constitutional theory;[21] it is a revolutionary concept that implies not the defence of the constitution (as in the right of resistance), but the radical contestation of the pre-existing order and the foundation of a different order, which arises in opposition to the past. However, Graeber has convincingly questioned the application of this concept to superheroes by arguing that:

> Insofar as there is a potential for constituent power then, it can only come from purveyors of violence. The supervillains and evil masterminds, when they are not merely indulging in random acts of terror, are always scheming of imposing a New World Order of some kind or another [...] *Superheroes resist this logic. They do not wish to conquer the world – if only because they are not monomaniacal or insane. As a result, they remain parasitical off the villains in the same way that police remain parasitical off criminals: without them, they'd have no reason to exist. They remain defenders of a legal and political system which itself seems to have come out of nowhere, and which, however faulty or degraded, must be defended, because the only alternative is so much worse.*[22] [emphasis added].

19 *Batman: The Dark Knight Returns* directed by Jay Oliva (2012–2013).
20 Giddens (see note 13): 767.
21 E. J. Sieyès, *Qu'est-ce que le Tiers état?* (Paris: Éditions du Boucher, 2002 [1789]).
22 D. Graeber, 'Batman and the Problem of Constituent Power', 8 October 2012, http://revoltlib.com/anarchism/the-utopia-of-rules-on-technology-stupidity/appendix-batman-and-the-problem-of-constituent/.

What does Batman represent in this horizon of prevailing lawlessness? It has been suggested that Batman represents civil disobedience[23] or the right to resist, two concepts often seen as related but theoretically distinguishable. However, civil disobedience implies non-violence, the acceptance of sanction and the punctual, non-systematic nature of norm violation (what Rawls called the 'fidelity to law').[24] These elements are not always present in Batman, who for sure uses violence and makes rule-breaking part of his brand while collaborating with the Gotham police. In some ways, Batman's actions remind us of a kind of right to resist, a concept that has also been codified in some constitutions. The German legal system is very clear, for example, in conceiving the right to resist as a last resort, which can be used 'if no other remedy is available'.[25] In other words, when institutions fail, individual citizens can attempt to save the system by resisting an external threat.

The codification of the right to resist has occurred in Europe, especially in contexts that are characterised by a totalitarian or authoritarian past: Article 21 of the Portuguese Constitution;[26] Article 23 of the Czech Constitution;[27] and Article 32 of the Slovak Constitution.[28] The right to resist has rediscovered importance in many Latin American countries as well. Provisions codifying such a right are exposed to the risk of interpretative abuses, as has been pointed out by Ginsburg, Lansberg-Rodriguez and Versteeg.[29] While Article

23 Tony Thornley, 'Review: Superheroic Civil Disobedience In 'Batman' #111', 9 August, https://comicon.com/2021/08/09/review-superheroic-civil-disobedience-in-batman-111/#:~:text=For%20large%20parts%20of%20the,and%20some%20great%20atmospheric%20colors..

24 On civil disobedience Rawls wrote that: 'It expresses disobedience to law within the limits of fidelity to law, although it is at the outer edge thereof. The law is broken, but fidelity to law is expressed by the public and nonviolent nature of the act, by the willingness to accept the legal consequences of one's conduct', J. Rawls, *A Theory of Justice* (Cambridge: Cambridge University Press, 2003): 322.

25 Article 20(4) of the German Basic Law: 'All Germans shall have the right to resist any person seeking to abolish this constitutional order if no other remedy is available'.

26 Article 21 of the Portuguese Constitution: 'Everyone has the right to resist any order that infringes their rights, freedoms or guarantees and, when it is not possible to resort to the public authorities, to use force to repel any aggression'.

27 Article 23 of the Czech Constitution: 'Citizens have the right to put up resistance to any person who would do away with the democratic order of human rights and fundamental freedoms established by this Charter, if the actions of constitutional institutions or the effective use of legal means have been frustrated'.

28 Article 32 of the Slovak Constitution: 'The citizens shall have the right to resist anyone who would abolish the democratic order of human rights and freedoms set in this Constitution, if the activities of constitutional authorities and the effective application of legal means are restrained'.

29 'Constitutions are typically adopted to bind the future on behalf of the present. Yet our findings show that they, at least in some cases, also have the important purpose of interpreting,

20(4) of the German Basic Law cannot be described as a post-totalitarian provision since it was introduced in 1968, in some cases the codification of the right of resistance is clearly a reaction to the abuses created by a totalitarian (or authoritarian) regime, which had passed laws that were in clear contrast with justice and dignity. However, not even the right to resist seems to be entirely applicable to the world of Batman.

Of course, in the scheme of the German Basic Law, the precondition of activating resistance as a last resort implies the (at least partial) failure of the institutions, but with the idea of returning the latter to full functioning. The Caped Crusader, instead, does not seem to be interested in the defence of institutions as such. While Batman's concept of justice extends beyond the pursuit of vengeance, his idea of justice is that of 'just punishment' ('just desert'[30]). In other words, beyond the punitive moment, Batman's 'politics of justice' is characterised by a lack of consideration of the wider institutional dimension. His world is defined by a corrupt system that is sustained by the continual violation of established rules.

Laws That Create Discrimination and Segregation

Comics also offer various examples of how law can be used to create discrimination and injustice. This reminds us of the need to distinguish between law and justice. In totalitarian regimes, laws have been passed that discriminated against minorities, just think of the horrible laws passed during Nazism and Fascism, but this unfortunately also often happens in supposedly democratic contexts. An obvious example of this is racial segregation, which has demonstrated the ambiguities present since its genesis in the political system we often consider democratic par excellence, namely that of the United States.

The comics offer many examples of discrimination based on laws passed in violation of the principle of equality, for example, those tending to marginalise and discriminate against mutants.

---

and in some cases justifying, the past. Finally, the conclusion explores the possible consequences of the right to resist in actual constitutional practice', T. Ginsburg, D. Lansberg-Rodriguez, and M. Versteeg, 'When to Overthrow your Government: The Right to Resist in the World's Constitutions', *UCLA Law Review* 60, no. 5 (2013): 1184–1260.

30 'By constituting himself as an agent of violence and retribution, skirting the periphery of the rule of law, Batman's actions clearly indicate that central to his ideology of justice is the notion of just desert', C. Sharp, 'Riddle Me This...?' Would the World Need Superheroes If the Law Could Actually Deliver 'Justice'?, *Law Text Culture* 16, no. 1 (2012): 353–378, 373.

In many cases, in these fictional universes, we learn of laws targeting superheroes or mutants. This is the case with the Registration Acts[31] in Marvel publisher's stories, the Keene Act in the Watchmen universe,[32] the Superhuman Registration Act in Marvel's Civil War events, or the Sokovia Accords in the Marvel Cinematic Universe. Very often we do not know much about these laws and in some cases they are bills that have not been passed, but only discussed or announced.

These discriminations are produced by passing laws that are clearly detrimental to the rights of these minorities and are perpetrated by politicians who can be described as populist because, in their rhetoric, they explicitly portray mutants (or superheroes) as a threat and something alien to the human race they represent.

Superhero stories are frequently also stories of the integration of subjects born on other planets and then ended up on planet Earth (Krypton in the case of *Superman* and Planet Vegeta in the case of Son Goku, the main character in *Dragon Ball* by Akira Toriyama). Often these characters carry a contradiction: their powers are seen as a gift, but also as a curse. Supervillains often reach planet Earth to confront them, and this sometimes causes them to be seen as the cause of the planet's problems. Not to mention the accidental damage created by superheroes in their battles.

In particular, *Days of Future Past*[33] by Chris Claremont is a masterpiece that offers many insights for constitutional law scholars[34] in this respect. In this storyline, Senator Robert Kelly is pushing for a law called the Mutant Control Act, which would require mutants to register and disclose their abilities to the government. The response to this proposed Act varies among mutants. Charles Xavier and his X-Men advocate for peaceful coexistence between humans and mutants, while the members of the Brotherhood of Mutants strongly opposes the Act. More generally, there are two different approaches to the issue of how to resolve the question of coexistence, and they are represented by Charles Xavier and Magneto:

---

31 For an overview see: Marvel [Database], 'Registration Acts', 26 October 2021, https://marvel.fandom.com/wiki/Registration_Acts#Superhuman_Registration_Act.

32 A. Reiher, 'A Guide to Watchmen's Senator Keene and the Keene Act', 28 October 2019, https://www.popsugar.com/entertainment/what-is-keene-act-on-watchmen-46803914.

33 *The Uncanny X-Men* (issues #141–142) by Chris Claremont and John Byrne, 1981.

34 For a detailed analysis of this story see: L. P. Vanoni, 'From Civil Rights to Identity Politics? Law and Diversity in the X-Men', in *The Law in Graphic Narratives. Legal Perspectives on Comics, Manga and Anime*, eds. G. Martinico and G. M. Ruotolo (Berlin: De Gruyter, 2024): 87–106.

> [T]he mutants of Stan Lee's X-Men represent opposing approaches in the battles for racial recognition, equality, and/or dominance. Mutants are a minority group born with supernatural powers – an inherent 'Otherness'. Humans hate and fear the mutants. Some of that is because of their 'Otherness'. Some of it is because of the existential threat that mutants pose to humans. For example, as mutant Magneto indicated: 'The human race no longer deserves dominion over the planet Earth! The day of the mutants is upon us! The first phase of my plan shall be to show my power [...] [*sic*] to make homo sapiens bow to homo superior!' The X-Men serve as a buffer between these two conflicting groups with the goal to attain mutant equality through peaceful measures yet are also willing to fight for their cause.[35]

In *Days of Future Past*, Senator Robert Kelly is killed by the Brotherhood of Evil Mutants and this produces political upheavals that lead to the election of an anti-mutant president, the approval of the Mutant Control Act and of a series of measures that will lead to the killing of many mutants and the creation of concentration camps. The law itself, however, is declared unconstitutional by the Supreme Court, likely due to the Equal Protection Clause enshrined in the Fourteenth Amendment. Whereas after the landmark *Brown v. Board of Education* decision,[36] which ended racial segregation, the federal authority decided to challenge the unruly States to make what the Supreme Court had ruled effective,[37] in this story the President and his majority challenge the authority of the Supreme Court with the apparent support of public opinion. Indeed, in spite of the ruling, the President of the United States decides to send Sentinels – a group of mutant-hunting robots – against the mutants.

However, a caveat is necessary here: obviously, the existence of a law designed to regulate the activities of super-powered individuals, in a context where super-powers are an exception,[38] is not per se illegitimate. Indeed,

35 G. S. Parks, Gregory, and M. W. Hughey, '"A Choice of Weapons": The X-Men and the Metaphor for Approaches to Racial Equality', *Indiana Law Journal* 92, no. 5 (2017): 1–26, 8. In this article, among other things, the authors analyse and challenge the Charles Xavier/Martin Luther King Jr and Magneto/Malcom X parallelism, Ibid.: 12–13.

36 US Supreme Court, Brown v. Board of Education of Topeka, 347 U.S. 483 (1954).

37 To mention a famous case of State disobedience, in September 1957, the Arkansas Governor used the Arkansas National Guard to prevent nine Afro-American students, later called the 'Little Rock Nine', from entering Little Rock Central High School after the decision of the US Supreme Court. In response, President Dwight D. Eisenhower took control of the State's National Guard and sent troops from the US Army's 101st Airborne Division to protect the students and ensure they could safely enter and attend school.

38 It would be different if the superheroes were more than a small minority, as in the case of the universe described in *My Hero Academia* by Kōhei Horikoshi. In this work, the story is set in a

providing procedures for the registration of super-powered individuals might also be necessary in order to understand how to respond to any damage caused by them. Of course, to be legitimate, these registration procedures would have to take into account other issues related to the security, secrecy and privacy of superheroes, especially those who do not want to reveal their true identity. This is therefore an issue of great interest, at least potentially.

Being a lawyer, I have to say that it would therefore be necessary to have a precise idea of the contents of the Mutant Control Act in order to understand whether the law in question produces real discrimination or introduces a reasonable distinction. Unfortunately, in *Days of Future Past*, nothing is said about the contents of the act at stake, but in the alternative future from which it comes, there are scenes that portray concentration camps,[39] so it certainly paved the way for forms of segregation and even worse.

The plot in *Days of Future Past* highlights the dangers of populist demagoguery and the risk of abuse of law according to dynamics that scholars have called 'abusive constitutionalism'[40] or 'autocratic legalism'.[41] When commenting on this storyline, Vanoni draws a parallel between the Mutant Control Act and the Jim Crow laws, which legalised and enforced racial segregation in the south of the United States. He also emphasised that Claremont himself explored themes of civil rights, government overreach and the manipulation of public sentiment, reflecting anxieties about discriminatory legislation and authoritarianism in his works.[42]

From the viewpoint of a constitutional law scholar, this makes *Days of Future Past* very intriguing, since it offers a perfect representation of how populists in power abuse the law to attack insular minorities.

It is possible to identify some elements that characterise populisms, namely extreme majoritarianism and 'identity politics',[43] since they are crucial to distinguishing the kind of democracy proposed by populists from that preserved in constitutional democracies. For the purpose of this chapter, I will

world where, as a consequence of a genetic mutation, the human species has acquired the capacity to develop superhuman abilities, designated as 'Quirk' in the fictional universe.

39 *The Uncanny X-Men* (issues #141–142) by Chris Claremont and John Byrne, 1981.

40 D. Landau, 'Abusive Constitutionalism', *UC Davies Law Review* 47, no. 1 (2013): 189–260.

41 K. Corrales, 'Autocratic Legalism in Venezuela', *Journal of Democracy* 26, no. 2 (2015): 37–51, 38; 'When electoral mandates plus constitutional and legal change are used in the service of an illiberal agenda, I call this phenomenon autocratic legalism', K. Lane Scheppele, 'Autocratic Legalism', *The University of Chicago Law Review*, 85, no. 2, (2018): 545–583, 548.

42 Vanoni (see note 34): 93–94.

43 G. Martinico, *Filtering Populist Claims to Fight Populism: The Italian Case in a Comparative Perspective* (Cambridge: Cambridge University Press, 2021).

focus on identity politics, which involves portraying the majority as a unified group endowed with moral superiority, in contrast to the elite, which is often depicted as corrupt. In other words, 'populists combine anti-elitism with a conviction that they hold a superior vision of what it means to be a true citizen of their nation'.[44] Indeed, populists advocate for a majoritarian concept of democracy,[45] which portrays anyone outside the majority as the 'others'. This dichotomous approach and the need for an enemy have led Müller to highlight the Schmittian undertones of populism.[46] In Schmitt, public law becomes part of a constitutional narrative that represents the people as forged by a static identity that goes back to the mythological origin of the legal system. This reconstruction is based on an organicistic reading of the concept of the people. This identitarian public law makes instrumental use of the moral argument, the historical argument and the religious argument. As Corrias suggested, 'the typical populist reading of identity in terms of sameness comes with (dubious) normative connotations, like the alleged purity of a national identity and the appointment of elements which are (supposedly) hostile to and thus a threat to this purity'.[47]

In so doing, populists appeal to a 'mythical Volksgemeinschaft',[48] create 'imagined communities'[49] and need 'walls' to mark a border between what they claim to be the 'real' people and others, and use the identity argument to exclude political competitors from the circle of legitimacy. In other words, the kind of majority described by populists tends not to be inclusive.

Once in power, the populists, if given the necessary numbers, have also tried to codify into a constitution the values that should characterise the people and have thus weaponised constitutional law, using it to discriminate against minorities who do not share those values.

There is no shortage of examples in comparative constitutional law. For example, this is the case with some provisions of the Russian Constitution of 1993, last amended in 2020. Article 67.1 (2) and (3), introduced in 2020,

---

44 M. Marchlewska, A. Cichocka, O. Panayiotou, K. Castellanos, and J. Batayneh, 'Populism as Identity Politics: Perceived In-Group Disadvantage, Collective Narcissism, and Support for Populism', *Social Psychological and Personality Science*, 9, no. 2 (2018): 151–162.

45 Y. Mény and Y. Surel, 'The Constitutive Ambiguity of Populism', in *Democracies and the Populist Challenge*, eds. Y. Mény and Y. Surel (London: Palgrave, 2022): 1–22, 19.

46 J. W. Müller, *What Is Populism?* (Philadelphia: University of Pennsylvania Press, 2017).

47 L. Corrias, 'Populism in a Constitutional Key: Constituent Power, Popular Sovereignty and Constitutional Identity', *European Constitutional Law Review*, 12, no. 1 (2016): 6–26.

48 J. Abromeit, 'Critical Review of Recent Literature on Populism', *Politics and Governance*, 5, no. 4 (2017): 177–186, 183.

49 B. Anderson, *Imagined Communities: Reflections on the Origin and Spread of Nationalism* (London: Verso, 1983).

provides that 'the Russian Federation, united by thousand-year history [...] The Russian Federation honors the memory of defenders of the Fatherland, provides protection of the *historical truth.* Diminution of the heroic deed of the people defending the Fatherland is precluded' [emphasis added]. This is also the case with Article R.4 of the Hungarian Basic Law, according to which, 'the protection of the *constitutional identity and Christian culture of Hungary* shall be an obligation of every organ of the State'[50] [emphasis added].

Courts, counter-majoritarian actors[51] par excellence, are often the target of attacks by ruling populists and are often accused of being anti-democratic actors. This is also a view that responds to a purely majoritarian view of democracy, which is reduced, in other words, to majority rule. It is important to clarify that, in this context, 'counter-majoritarian' should not be interpreted as anti-democratic or opposed to democracy. This distinction is crucial to avoid, again, reducing democracy to mere majority rule. Democracy is a more complex concept, in which the majority has the right to govern, but this right is contingent upon safeguarding the equality of citizens and the pluralism of ideas. Therefore, concrete protections for minorities are essential to the functioning of a true democracy.[52] This means that counter-majoritarian actors are not an exception to democracy; rather, they are essential democratic actors[53] to preserve pluralism. Precisely because the courts, especially

50 'The defining characteristic of the Hungarian Fundamental Law is its strong constitutional identity: the political identity of the supermajority has become constitutionalized. This identity image has a number of positive elements (i.e., elements that have been defined as desirable, a kind of fundamental characteristic of the public law system). These include Christianity, active memory politics, national cohesion, various aspects of sustainability [...] in addition to the explicitly strong positive constitutional identity elements, the constitutional power intended that negative identity elements should be at least as strong as the positive ones (in many ways even stronger and more important in the daily political struggles relying constitutional identity) [...] the negative constitutional identity has been presented in the original constitutional conception, which started to unfold in 2010, but also since 2015 (embedded in the amendments to the Fundamental Law) the constitutional enemy formation pervades public law and political debates. Three basic strands of Constitutionalised Image of Enemy (CIE) have emerged (and this reflects the constitution-power's view of history and the past): (1) antiCommunism framed in actual political framework; (2) anti-immigration; (3) anti-gender as the opposition to non-heterosexual forms of coexistence', A. Antal, 'The Constitutionalised Image of Enemy in the Hungarian Fundamental Law', *iCourts Working Paper Series*, no. 311, 2022, https://papers.ssrn.com/sol3/papers.cfm?abstract_id=4287382.

51 On the counter-majoritarian difficulty of courts, see: A. Bickel, *The Least Dangerous Branch* (New Haven: Yale University Press, 1986).

52 H. Kelsen, *Vom Wesen und Wert der Demokratie* (Tübingen: J.B.C. Mohr, 1929): 61.

53 'By applying public reason the court is to prevent that law from being eroded by the legislation of transient majorities, or more likely, by organised and well situated narrow interests skilled

those with the power to declare majority laws unconstitutional, are often seen as targets of populists, the latter in illiberal contexts normally seek to undermine their independence by making judges, tools in the hands of the executive.[54] This has happened in Hungary, in Poland and, according to many, is what has also happened with the Supreme Court under Donald Trump's presidency.

Final Remarks

In this chapter, I have reflected on the pathological side of law and, to do so, I thought of using comics and, in particular, of focusing on the iconic figures of Batman and the X-Men to analyse the theme of unjust laws as a privileged perspective to reflect on two issues: the insufficiency of law and the use of law as a tool to create discrimination and segregation.

As mentioned, these are only a few possible paths, but they show the usefulness that comics can have in teaching and legal research through the medium of comics.

Obviously, similar thematic itineraries can also be developed using *manga*, *bande desinné* or other forms of graphic narratives, and this is particularly interesting for those studying comparative law. Indeed, in each of these graphic narratives, the law is portrayed in a way that reflects the culture of the authors' homeland. This implies the need for a double contextualisation: on the one hand, it is necessary to take into account the fictional universe of the comic book or manga taken into consideration, but also that of the legal culture from which the author was inspired when representing legal dynamics.

---

at getting their way. If the court assumes this role and effectively carries it out, it is incorrect to say that it is straight-forwardly antidemocratic', J. Rawls, *Political Liberalism* (New York: Columbia University Press, 2005): 233–234.

54 On this phenomenon in Europe, see P. Castillo-Ortiz, 'The Illiberal Abuse of Constitutional Courts in Europe', *European Constitutional Law Review*, 15, no. 1 (2019): 48–72.

Chapter 4

FROM POP CULTURE TO WOKE CULTURE? LAW AND POLITICS IN THE X-MEN SAGA

Luca Pietro Vanoni*

Comics, Politics and Law

In a viral interview with Syfy.com, comic book writer Kelly Sue DeConnick addressed fan criticism regarding the alleged 'woke' political turns in her comics: 'I'm sorry to break it to you, but Captain America is a social justice warrior. I understand you mean that as an insult, but that's exactly what he is.'[1]

The topic is not brand new. We live in highly polarised times, and comics make no exceptions. Some people are calling for greater diversity and inclusion, urging a 'cultural awakening' in society to address social justice, inequity and systemic discrimination. Grounded in academic studies like Critical Race Theory, terms such as 'woke culture' or 'wokeness' have become familiar in public discourse and media. The term originally emerged in the early twentieth century to describe an awareness of the sociopolitical challenges facing Black Americans. However, in recent decades, it has evolved significantly, gaining broader meaning and influence, impacting journalism, advertising and visual arts. Entertainment companies sometimes actively promote this message, integrating it directly into their movies or TV shows. As highlighted by the Disney website, 'stories matter' because they 'shape how we see ourselves and everyone around us. So as storytellers, we have the power and responsibility to not only uplift and inspire, but also consciously, purposefully

---

* All websites accessed on 12 November 2024.

1 K. S. DeConnick, 'SYFY WIRE Interview', 18 November 2017, https://www.youtube.com/watch?v=sIdgTGAaBB8.

and relentlessly champion the spectrum of voices and perspectives in our world'.

According to proponents, this policy could lead to a new form of storytelling that challenges conventional norms and highlights the struggles of underrepresented communities. In comics, for example, it has recently altered the narratives of traditional and beloved characters such as Superman, Captain Marvel, Spider-Man and Captain America, changing aspects of their origins, race or gender.[2] However, especially in the United States, this shift has sparked strong reactions from more traditional segments of society, fuelling what some describe as a 'culture of complaint', which deepens societal tribalism.[3] While some advocate for greater diversity in comics, others express concern, arguing that such changes could lead to the desecration of traditional heroes. Sometimes, this clash also leads to social campaigns aimed at boycotting or ostracising specific companies, with some fans expressing frustration by asking, 'Would you please get *your* politics out of *my* comic books?' However, DeConnick argued, comic books have always been political: 'What comic books are you reading?!' she responded, 'Where are the *apolitical* comic books?'[4]

In this chapter, I will explore the relationship between law, politics and identity within the X-Men saga in the Marvel Universe. Originally created in 1963 by Stan Lee and Jack Kirby, the X-Men are superheroes whose abilities stem from a genetic mutation. Unlike other classic superheroes, the X-Men are viewed by humans with suspicion and prejudice, as the same X-Gene that grants them superhuman abilities also marks them as 'different'.

The central theme of the X-Men comic is the clash between *Homo sapiens* and *Homo superior*, and the ongoing tension between inclusion and exclusion of otherness. Over the sixty years of their saga, the X-Men have consistently been viewed as a paradigm of diversity, integration and nondiscrimination. This makes the X-Men a compelling case study for examining the intersection of law, politics and comics and how they mutually influence one another.

---

2 As explained by the DC Editor Tom Taylor, commenting his decision to introduce in the DC Universe a new Superman who is concerned about the environment, does not shy away from politics, and is in a romantic relationship with a male friend, 'I've always said everyone needs heroes and they deserve to see themselves in their heroes. For so many people, having the strongest superhero in comics come out is incredibly powerful'. See G. G. Gustine, 'Superman Comes Out, as DC Comics Ushers In a New Man of Steel', *New York Times*, 11 October 2021, https://www.nytimes.com/2021/10/11/arts/superman-comes-out.html.

3 R. Huges, *Culture of Complaint: A Passionate Look into the Ailing Heart of America* (New York: Oxford University Press, 1994).

4 K. S. DeConnick (see note 1).

The Origin of the Mutant Metaphor: Diversity *as* Complexity

Since their inception, comic books have been deeply entwined with politics, and even the idea of narrating the political struggle for the recognition of diversity through comics was not invented by the X-Men.

From the very beginning of the American comics industry, DC Comics used Superman to express the values and ideals of American identity. Superman's origin follows the exploits of an alien who has fallen to Earth and dedicates himself to protecting humanity. Beyond the obvious messianic parallel, Superman's narrative also serves as an allegory for the immigrant experience. In the late 1930s, comic book writers used Superman's comics to show immigrants 'the skills they would need to succeed in their new lives as American citizens',[5] helping to facilitate their integration into society. In the Marvel Universe, Captain America stands as a powerful symbol of the American Dream and patriotic political narratives. Created during World War II, the character was designed to embody the ideals of freedom, justice and democracy, reflecting the aspirations of the American people. With his iconic shield and star-spangled uniform, Captain America became a tool of American propaganda, particularly during wartime, fighting against Nazis, Soviets, terrorists and every other enemy of the American people.

During the 1960s, particularly with the rise of the American Civil Rights Movement and the political struggle for the recognition of African American rights, many comics sought to reflect this fight for equality by creating new heroes with whom racial minorities could identify. Superheroes such as Black Panther and Falcon were invented to represent Black communities' demands for recognition and the broader social struggle for racial equality. Both assume a classic narrative pattern to represent the otherness they embody, but particularly Black Panther symbolises 'the proud African heritage from which he derives his powers'[6] and jealously protects his otherness from a corrupt society. However, by recounting traditions far removed from the lives of African American readers, he lacked the authenticity necessary to effectively represent the struggles for vindication the Civil Rights Movement underwent during those years.

The X-Men profoundly differed from the approach used by Black Panther's writers. In an interview that appeared in *The Guardian* in 2000, Stan Lee recalled some of his stylistic motivations for the X-Men superheroes:

5 L. A. Woodall III, 'The Secret Identity of Race: Exploring Ethnic and Racial Portrayals in Superhero Comic Books', *Dissertations,* 478 (2010): 1–217, 70, https://aquila.usm.edu/dissertations/478.

6 L. A. Woodall III (see note 5), 166.

> [I]t occurred to me that instead of them just being heroes that everybody admired, what if I made other people fear and suspect and actually hate them because they were different? I loved that idea; it not only made them different, but it was a good metaphor for what was happening with the Civil Rights Movement in the country at that time.[7]

The decision to shape the X-Men through the lens of contemporary American sociopolitical movements produced significant sociological, political and narrative outcomes.

First and foremost, the characters created by Stan Lee in X-Men introduce the theme of complexity in the process of public recognition of identities. Unlike characters that individually embody a certain concept of otherness, the X-Men are a group of individuals with abilities, characteristics and significantly different profiles, who are united by being mutants. Narratively, this insight allows Lee and Kirby to construct an almost infinite set of characters. Sociologically, this plot device introduces the concept of 'multiple identities'[8] within X-Men comics and with it, the inner conflict between the identities of its characters.

This original vision of Lee and Kirby was further developed by Chris Claremont in the 1970s, when the complexity of the X-Men characters reached its full potential. Claremont's work deepened the characterization, adding layers of nuance and emotional depth, which allowed the series to fully explore not only the conflicts between mutants and humans but also the internal struggles within the mutant community itself.

A quick review of the X-Men heroes highlights these striking contrasts. Charles Xavier, the X-Men's founder, is the most powerful telepath on the planet, yet he has spent many years bound to a wheelchair. His main antagonist, Magneto, has the ability to control magnetic fields, but he is also a persecuted Jew and a Holocaust survivor, having first experienced the traumatic manifestation of his powers in Auschwitz. Scott Summers, aka Cyclops, has the ability to fire destructive optic beams from his eyes, but he is forced to wear quartz-ruby glasses to control them. Piotr Nikolayevich Rasputin, or Colossus, is a Russian mutant who can turn his body into metal. Raised on a Soviet collective farm, he experiences discrimination due to his political views. Kurt Wagner, also known as Nightcrawler, is a devout Catholic,

---

7 B. Strauss, 'Generator X', *The Guardian*, 12 August 2000, https://www.theguardian.com/film/2000/aug/12/features.

8 See B. Scheuringer, *Multiple Identities: A Theoretical and an Empirical Approach* (Cambridge: Cambridge University Press, 2016).

and in one storyline becomes a priest. His mutation grants him the ability to teleport, but it also alters his appearance, turning him into a blue-skinned, devil-like figure. Ironically, despite his faith, he is feared by many within his own religion because of his demonic appearance.

These characters (along with many others) testify to the inevitable tension between the self as an individual and the self as part of a social group: disability, ethnicity, political views and religion, thus, become the individual identities that, intertwining with the shared *mutant diversity*, contribute to enriching the prism of otherness. These elements transform the X-Men mutants into the image of the existential human struggle for the fulfilment of the desire for public recognition and the search for an authentic and complete identity.[9]

Although stigmatised and gathered in a deviant community, the X-Men aspire to join American society, whose norms and values they intend to protect through their fights. Professor Xavier dreams 'to bring mankind and its mutant children together in peace and harmony',[10] and the X-Men 'fight to protect a world that hates and fears them'.[11] Professor Xavier's vision involves not only protecting mutants from human prejudice but also educating society to accept mutants and for mutants to protect society in return.[12] This idealistic dream, however, directly clashes with the vision of Xavier's nemesis, Magneto, the leader of the Brotherhood of Evil Mutants. Magneto believes that mutants must use their powers 'to make *homo sapiens* bow to *homo superior*',[13] reclaiming their dominion over Earth. This fundamental conflict between peaceful coexistence and domination has defined the core ideological struggle of the X-Men universe from the very first encounter between Magneto and Xavier:

> *Magneto:* 'Only you and your X Men stand between the mutants and the world conquest! Why! Why do you fight us?' For *you too* are mutant!!
> *Professor Xavier:* 'But I seek to save mankind, not destroy it! [...] We must use our powers to bring about a Golden Age on Earth [...] side by side with ordinary humans'.[14]

9 S. Petruccioli, *Gli X-Men e la Filosofia* (Milan: Mimesis Edizioni, 2014).
10 Classic X-Men #23 (1978).
11 J. J. Darowski, *X-Men and the Mutant Metaphor: Race and Gender in the Comic Books* 34 (Lanham, MD: Rowman & Littlefield, 2014).
12 J. J. Darowski, *The Ages of the X-Men* (Jefferson: McFarland & Company, Inc., Publishers, Kindle ed., 2020).
13 X-Men #1 (Sept 1963) by Stan Lee: Magneto: 'The human race no longer deserves dominion over the planet Earth! The day of the mutants is upon us! The first phase of my plan shall be to show my power [...] to make Homo sapiens bow to Homo superior!'
14 X-Men #4 (March 1964) by Stan Lee.

Over time, this dialogue has resonated throughout the pages of X-Men comic books, becoming a cornerstone of the entire saga and setting the foundation for its ongoing themes and narrative rules. More importantly, it reflects the complexity within the Civil Rights Movement, making the series a powerful metaphor for real-world conflicts and cultural tensions:

> Specifically, the methods in X-Men mirror those of the civil rights movement: Dr. Xavier and the X-Men represent the peaceful embrace of 'Otherness', as articulated via the integrationist movement; Magneto and his army represent the more aggressive battle to strengthen 'Otherness', as promoted by the black militant/nationalist movements.[15]

Throughout the years, and especially when Chris Claremont departed from the traditional hero-versus-villain canon, building towards a climactic relationship/clash between Professor Xavier and Magneto, these two main characters came to be seen as metaphors for Civil Rights leaders Martin Luther King Jr and Malcolm X, respectively. Despite some inaccuracies in the analogy,[16] the parallel between Professor X and Dr Martin Luther King Jr, and Magneto and Malcolm X, has been studied as a fair representation of the two strategies present in the Civil Rights Movement.[17]

Thanks to this allegory, the comic was able to represent the struggle for civil rights recognition in all its complexity. Though caricatured, the juxtaposition of Magneto as Malcolm X and Xavier as Martin Luther King is capable of showcasing, in its infinite nuances, an ongoing ideological conflict still present in American society to this day. This conflict is perhaps best captured in a dialogue between Magneto and Xavier's pupil, Cyclops, penned by Chris Claremont several years later:

> *Magneto:* 'I am not your enemy, X-Men, nor do I consider you mine. True, my goal has ever been the conquest of earth – but solely to create a world where our race, Homo Superior, can live in peace. Look at yourselves, risking your lives for a humanity that would rather see you behind bars, or dead. Why do you persist?'
> *Cyclops:* 'Is your way any better? A mutant dictatorship?'

---

15 G. S. Parks, Gregory, and M. W. Hughey, '"A Choice of Weapons": The X-Men and the Metaphor for Approaches to Racial Equality', *Indiana Law Journal* 92, no. 5 (2017): 1–26, 8–9.
16 See Mikhail Lyubansky, 'Prejudice Lessons from the Xavier Institute', in *The Psychology Of Superheroes: An Unauthorized Exploration*, 75, eds. R. S. Rosenberg and J. Canzonieri (Dallas TX: Benbella Books INC., 2008).
17 G. S. Parks, Gregory and M. W. Hughey (see note 15).

Magneto: 'Do not take that tone with me boy. I have lived under a dictatorship and seen my family butchered by its servants. When I rule, it will be for the betterment of all. Contentment breeds tranquility – discontent, rebellion. Therefore, I shall ensure the one by eliminating the root causes of the other: hunger, poverty, disease, war. The freedoms lost will not be noticed, even in the most libertarian of states. And the material benefits should more than balance the scales'.[18]

Evidence of this continued struggle is seen today in police brutality against people of colour and the emergence of the Black Lives Matter movement. The dilemma between asserting identity and otherness versus integration into society remains very much alive in America, along with the strategies used to fight for these issues: as stated during the tragic uprising in Ferguson, Missouri, 'Violence works. Nonviolence does too'.[19]

Expanding the Metaphor: Sex and Bigotry in Claremont's X-Men Run

Although the mutant metaphor was originally conceived by Lee and Kirby, the full expansion of the idea and the true success of the saga are largely credited to the British writer Chris Claremont. Lee and Kirby's X-Men had its moment, but in 1975, when Claremont took over writing Uncanny X-Men, the series had just been rebooted after a five-year hiatus due to poor sales. During his 16-year run, X-Men became a worldwide phenomenon, probably because they faced greater prejudice than they experienced in the first decades, allowing Claremont to exploit the mutant metaphor to its full potential.

To achieve this goal, Claremont gradually added, replaced or evolved the original team of WASPish, middle- to upper-class X-Men with new members from diverse races, genders and nationalities. This diversification of the team reflected a broader vision, allowing the X-Men to represent a wider range of identities. More importantly, Claremont demonstrated a unique sensitivity in character development, both in terms of their inner narrative arcs and their connection to the sociopolitical and legal context, allowing his characters to evolve in ways that reflected real-world struggles. This depth in storytelling made the X-Men more than just a superhero saga – it became a thoughtful

---

18 *God Loves, Man Kills* by C. Claremont and B. Anderson (ed., 1994).

19 T. Coates, 'Barack Obama, Ferguson, and the Evidence of Things Unsaid', *The Atlantic*, 26 November 2014, https://perma.cc/6W2P-52C6.

commentary on the complexities of the human experience, particularly regarding identity, discrimination and justice.

Law, politics and constitutional history played a significant role in Claremont's storytelling. One of the reasons for his success was the introduction of strong female characters as central figures in his narratives, breaking away from the traditional, limited roles accorded to women in 1960s comic books. Instead of being limited to the token supporting roles traditionally allotted to women, Claremont's female heroes were complex, powerful and integral to the narrative. In the first generation of X-Men, despite her superpowers, Marvel Girl (aka Jean Grey) was often relegated to the helpless damsel-in-distress role. Depicting a radical transformation, Claremont turned Jean Grey's character from

> [a] sort of very preppy, Republican, restrained 'oh my gosh she looks like she just stepped out of Neiman Marcus' figure [...] [into] a more independent and dynamic figure [...].[20]

In Claremont's hands, Jean's powers were not only brought up to the same level as the male characters but beyond, as she became Phoenix, the most powerful being in the galaxy.[21] In the iconic *The Dark Phoenix Saga*, Jean Grey was possessed by the Phoenix Force, a cosmic entity and mutable manifestation of the prime universal force of life.[22] The Phoenix eventually corrupted Jean, turning her into a formidable threat to the universe. However, Jean's strong moral values and willingness to sacrifice herself ultimately allowed her to defeat the Dark Phoenix, saving the world and the lives of her beloved friends. Depicting a Shakespearean narrative arc, Claremont transformed the archetypal team girl into the star of one of the most beloved storylines in superhero fiction. Most notably, Claremont's affinity for female characters did not primarily rely on a stereotypical girl empowerment strategy, but on an intelligent observation of real life. As he revealed in an interview,

> My attitude basically was, I have known a tremendous number of very courageous, very independent, very no-holds-barred, no-foolin' women, starting – cliché as it sounds – with my mom, who spent her college years in the Royal Air Force as part of a radar station on the south coast of England. [...] I look

---

20 C. Kaye, 'Why The Best X-Men Are X-Women', *Refinery29*, 20 May 2014, https://www.refinery29.com/en-us/2014/05/68147/x-men-feminism.

21 *Uncanny X-Men* (issues #104–108) by Chris Claremont and John Byrne, 1981.

22 *Uncanny X-Men* (issues #129–137) by Chris Claremont and John Byrne, 1981.

> at their lives and none of them are shy, withdrawn, secondary people. They are fierce, intelligent, courageous, gifted, heroic – in many respects – members of the community. And, I figured, 'Heck, my job as a writer is to give them a presence in my work, which is the X-Men'.[23]

This attitude helps Claremont to move away from the simplistic feminist dichotomy of sexist fear versus female empowerment, instead capturing the full complexity of the women he wrote. All the female characters he introduces in the team (such as Storm, Dazzler, Jubilee, Kitty Pryde, Rogue and many others) were intelligent, sexy, powerful, fun, emotional and, in a word, human. One clear example of this approach is the narrative arc of the Black woman Ororo Munroe (Storm). Worshipped as a goddess in Africa because of her ability to control weather, Storm was designed to stand out from previous super-women and not only by dint of her race or sex. From the very beginning, Storm was a strong and powerful hero, capable of summoning raging winds and deadly lightning strikes, and she quickly became one of the few characters with a consistently prominent presence throughout Claremont's entire 16-year run. Perhaps her most intriguing narrative arc was written during the 1980s, when she lost all her powers yet still managed to become the first female leader of the X-Men, defeating the team's historic leader, Cyclops.[24] This arc proved Storm's leadership and resilience extended far beyond her supernatural abilities, with even her new appearance – marked by a punky mohawk hairstyle – reflecting a physical manifestation of her complexity.[25]

Claremont's approach to realty shines also through his skillful incorporation of social, political and constitutional themes within his storylines. In *Days of Future Past*, Claremont portrays a bleak future where massive robots called Sentinels enforce a brutal regime of racial segregation against mutants. Mutants are systematically hunted, killed or imprisoned in sprawling detention camps, with their faces branded with an 'M' to mark their identity. This branding recalls historical symbols of persecution, such as the yellow Star of David forced upon Jews during the Holocaust, drawing powerful parallels between fictional oppression and real-world histories of marginalization.

Celebrated as a cornerstone of time travel dystopian science fiction, *Days of Future Past* offers layers of interpretation, with Claremont constructing its narrative around fictional legal issues that mirror real constitutional events. The

23 C. Kaye (see note 19).

24 *Uncanny X-Men* #201 by Chris Claremont and Rick Leonardi, 1981.

25 See A. Wheeler, 'Mutant Women of Earth: How Chris Claremont Reinvented the Female Superhero', 19 February 2013, https://comicsalliance.com/chris-claremont-x-men-strong-female-characters-storm-rogue-jean-grey/?utm_source=tsmclip&utm_medium=referral.

storyline opens with the introduction of the Mutant Control Act, a (fictional) federal law requiring mandatory registration of mutants. Although the US Supreme Court later declared the Act unconstitutional – likely on grounds of violating the Equal Protection Clause of the Fourteenth Amendment – the judicial battle intensified anti-mutant sentiment among the human population. This escalating tension led to the election of an anti-mutant president, who started the Sentinel Program to detect and eliminate the mutant threat. The Mutant Control Act allegorically echoes the Jim Crow Laws, just as the Supreme Court's fictional decision recalls the controversies generated by the *Dred Scott v. Sandford* (1857)[26] and the political consequences that led to the election of President Lincoln. In sum, as Giuseppe Martinico argued in a chapter of this book, '*Days of Future Past* offers many insights for constitutional law scholars',[27] since Claremont uses constitutional conflict between a federal law and Supreme Court scrutiny as a narrative tool useful to explain the authoritarian drift.

God Loves, Man Kills. Religious Fundamentalism and Critical Race Theory

Perhaps Claremont's most intriguing parallel between American sociopolitical conflicts and X-Men storytelling is drawn in the graphic novel *God Loves, Man Kills*, which extends the theme of discrimination – and the mutant's metaphor – to the thorny theme of religious extremism. Widely regarded as Claremont's masterpiece, the graphic novel introduces Reverend William Stryker, a former military officer and televangelist determined to pursue his anti-mutant crusade by any means necessary. His hatred for *homo superior* has a deep and personal root, a source of determination that drives him to create the sect of the Purifiers and devise a Machiavellian plan to convince the US Senate to support his policies. But, even more significantly, Stryker's crusade is fuelled by his evangelical faith, which strengthens his conviction that mutants are not children of God but genetic aberrations. In a sermon delivered before a massive crowd, Reverend Stryker preaches

> Are we now to let those who put forward the proposition that we are descended from apes tell us that *our* descendants – our *children* – will be born *monsters?!* And this is *natural?!?* I say NO! I say NEVER! We are as God made us! Any deviation from that sacred template – any *mutation* – comes not from heaven, but hell![28]

26 60 U.S. (19 How.) 393 (1857)

27 G. Martinico, *Law and Justice in Comics. An Itinerary*, in this volume, chapter 3, 25.

28 *God Loves, Man Kills* by C. Claremont and B. Anderson (ed., 1994)

Through the character of Reverend Stryker, Claremont staged the so-called 'return of religions in public space'[29] explored by Jose Casanova, reflecting the rise of evangelical preaching in the United States and particularly in the so-called Bible Belt States. Claremont read the Bible cover to cover more than once to get inspiration and travelled throughout the Country, spending Sunday after Sunday listening to media ministers both local and national. As noted by Claremont in the very introduction of the 2004 edition of the graphic novel,

> [In the 1980s] [T]here were a coterie of TV evangelists, trumpeting their born-again fundamentalist vision of the Bible across the national airwaves [...]. The vision of many of these ministries espoused was pure and focused. The Bible was not the font of wisdom, it was the path to salvation, not only for their souls of the individual parishioners, but through those individuals for the nation itself. [...] To me, it also seemed from an outsider perspective to be increasingly exclusionary. Other faiths, other branches of the same faith, sounded as they were being dismissed, which carries disturbing echoes of the growing fundamentalist movement that was sweeping the Islamic world. [...] [T]hese ministers were beginning to advance a broad-based social and political agenda, hoping to reshape the national landscape in terms of their faith.[30]

Within the pages of the comic book, Striker manipulates religion to incite hatred towards the mutant race, employing subtle methods and exploiting the media to amplify people's fears. Claremont's genius lies in using the social portrait of an America still deeply divided along racial lines as a narrative backdrop, intertwining it with the nation's traditionally religious spirit. The comic book thus anticipates the populist demagogic strategy of using religion as identity politics, where it becomes 'a matter of belonging rather than believing'.[31] Claremont skilfully highlights how religion can be manipulated for political purposes, emphasising the sense of belonging to a certain group based on religious affiliation rather than genuine belief. This exploration of the intersection between religion and identity politics remains relevant in today's society.

Alongside *Days of The Future Past*, the graphic novel *God Loves, Man Kills* was celebrated by sociologists as a turning point of the X-Men saga:

---

29 J. Casanova, *Public Religions in the Modern World* (Chicago: Chicago University Press, 1994)

30 *Introduction, God Loves, Man Kills* by C. Claremont and B. Anderson (ed., 1994)

31 R. Brubaker, 'Between Nationalism and Civilizationism: The European Populist Moment in Comparative Perspective', *Ethnic and Racial Studies*, 40, no. 8 (2017): 1191–1226.

> These stories are considered milestones because they finally brought the conversation of fundamental, systemic racism to the fore. [They] recognize that racism is deeply rooted and embedded in the structures of contemporary society [...] [T]he fundamental religious ideologies of William Stryker and the Purifiers, who terrorize and murder mutants just for being mutants (a comic version of the Ku Klux Klan) [...] point to the fundamental problems of societal and structural racism.[32]

This judgement directly links X-Men to Critical Race Theory (CRT), an academic movement developed in the early 1980s by legal scholars Derrick Bell and Richard Delgado. The core of the theory rests on the idea that race is a social construct and that racism is not solely the result of individual bias or prejudice but is also embedded in legal systems and policies. It emerged out of postmodernist theory, which tends to be sceptical of the ideas of universal values, objective knowledge, individual merit, Enlightenment rationalism and liberalism. As stated by R. Delgado in *Critical Race Theory: An Introduction*,

> Unlike traditional civil rights, which embraces incrementalism and step-by-step progress, critical race theory questions the very foundations of the liberal order, including equality theory, legal reasoning, Enlightenment rationalism, and neutral principles of constitutional law[33]

Although it was heavily criticised by historian[34] and legal[35] scholars, this theory became influential in education and was recently revitalised by writers like Robin DiAngelo, evolving into both a really popular and highly contested phenomenon.[36]

---

32 M. Dando, 'Black Heroes Matter: Toward a Critical Race Theory Framework for Comics Education' *Research on Diversity in Youth Literature*, 5, no. 1 (2022): 9–10.

33 R. Delgado and J. Stefancic, *Critical Race Theory. An Introduction* (New York: New York University Press, 2017): 3

34 Among others, see the letter written by Carol Berkin, Richard D. Brown, Jane E. Calvert, Joseph J. Ellis, Jack N. Rakove, and Gordon S. Wood, https://medium.com/@RichardDBrownCT/on-1619-and-woody-holtons-account-of-slavery-and-the-independence-movement-six-historians-respond-b43369ad52d7, contesting the '1619 Project', an ongoing initiative from The New York Times Magazine aims to reframe the Country's history by placing the consequences of slavery and the contributions of Black Americans at the very centre of our national narrative.

35 Douglas E. Litowitz, 'Some Critical Thoughts on Critical Race Theory', *Notre Dame Law Review*, 72, no. 2 (1997): 503–530, 505: 'in many cases CRT takes an approach that embodies fundamental errors or confusions about the proper role of argumentation within the law and the proper methodology of legal scholarship'

36 See R. Diangelo, *White Fragility* (Beacon Press: New York, 2018).

Even though it is grounded in academic studies, the link between CRT and Claremont's mutant metaphor is inaccurate, sloppy and ultimately deeply flawed.

First, Claremont's criticism is not aimed at religion as a structural social construct of the dominant society, but rather its personal, instrumental use. The graphic novel stigmatises William Stryker and his political and moral exploitation of religion, highlighting his attempt to reshape the national landscape according to the dictates of faith in a singular leader. As Claremont himself explained in the introduction of the comic books

> [United States] is a nation 'under God', but the definition of what 'God' represents is left open. It is, I always believed, to embrace a broad spectrum of faiths, whether held by a single individual or by tens of millions [...] William Stryker acted from his own perception of his faith. Yet at the same time, the people he was acting against were also – and remains – people of faith themselves. Is Nightcrawler's faith in the divine any less valid because Stryker believe him a creature of the Devil? And if Nightcrawler's faith is valid and true, what then of Stryker's condemnation?[37]

Secondly, Claremont's vision of faith and religion differs radically from the CRT approach because it is rooted in individual conscience and free will, linking moral and political responsibility to personal choices. Once again, Claremont's words dismiss the CRT approach:

> The graphic novel as evolved in a plea that, no matter what the dictates of faith, we must all be bound by our conscience as individuals. That to me is the nature of free will. We come to a point of choice, both in term of our faith as moral beings as our lives as good citizens. [...] Faith lies at the most fundamental core of our existence as sentient creatures, this need to believe in something greater than ourselves, this almost inherent acknowledgment of the miracle of creation. But as faith is personal ad unique to us as individuals, we the must also be our acceptance of responsibility for those actions that derive form it. Because in the end, while we remain individuals, we reside in a community. [...] We need to cherish that what binds us, and accept with a measure of tolerance some of the things that make us different.[38]

37 *Introduction, God Loves, Man Kills* by C. Claremont and B. Anderson (ed., 1994).

38 *Introduction, God Loves, Man Kills* by C. Claremont and B. Anderson (ed., 1994).

Perhaps the most compelling argument against the CRT approach is illustrated by Claremont in the graphic novel's conclusion. While there is a lot of action in the story, the final conflict between the X-Men and William Stryker is a battle of philosophical ideas. The X-Men arrive at Stryker's rally at Madison Square Garden, planning to rescue Xavier (whom Stryker has kidnapped and drugged to power a machine designed to kill all mutants) and to try to defuse the situation. They quickly realise that the real danger isn't the Purifiers or the machine, but rather Stryker's ideas themselves. Cyclops then directly challenges Stryker:

> *Cyclops:* 'What make your link with Heaven any stronger than mine? We have unique gifts […] but no more so, and more special than those granted a physician or physicist, or philosopher, or athlete. It could be due to an accident of nature or divine providence, who's to say? Are arbitrarily labels more important than the way we live our lives, what we are supposed to be more important than what we actually are?!' 'I hope I can be half the person he is. And if I have to choose between caring for my friend and believing in your God […] then I choose […] m-my friend! For all you know, we can be the real human race […] and the rest of you, the mutans'.
> *Stryker [pointing at Nightcrawler]:* '*Human?!* You dare calling that […] thing […] *HUMAN?!?*'[39]

In the climax of the event, Kitty Pride (once again: a woman and a Jewish) stands up for her friend and cries out:

> *Kitty:* 'MORE human than you! […] I hope I can be half person he is and if I have to choose between caring for my friend and believing in your God […] than I choose […] m-my fiends!'
> *Stryker [taking out a gun from his pocket]:* 'let those blasphemous worlds, girl […] be your epitaph'.[40]

Eventually, Stryker is shot and disarmed by a police officer at the Garden just before he can hit Kitty. One of Stryker's followers, astonished, exclaims, 'That cop – shot the Reverend!' The officer calmly replies, 'Yup – who was about to shoot an unarmed little girl. If that's the word of God, it's sure changed since Sunday school'.[41] Once again, Claremont reminds us that the

39 *God Loves, Man Kills* by C. Claremont and B. Anderson (ed., 1994).
40 *God Loves, Man Kills* by C. Claremont and B. Anderson (ed., 1994).
41 *God Loves, Man Kills* by C. Claremont and B. Anderson (ed., 1994).

difference between good and evil, between tolerance and bigotry, is ultimately a matter of individual character, free will and personal choice. Ironically, this message was delivered by a member of the police, often cited by critical race scholars as an example of systemic racism.

X-Men and Postmodernity: The Rise of Nationalism and Identity Politics

After Claremont's run concluded in 1991, the comic book was entrusted to a series of talented writers who expanded the saga's horizon in many directions. From the *Age of Apocalypse* (1995) to Grant Morrison's *New X-Men* (2001), the series explored a wide range of complex themes, leading the heroes to face increasingly dire threats – including a devastating mass genocide in *House of M* (2005). Despite these evolving storylines, the moral tension between striving for peaceful coexistence between humans and mutants and the bitter realisation that such a dream may be utopian or unattainable has remained a constant theme. While iconic characters like Magneto and Xavier have been reinterpreted multiple times – occasionally even exchanging roles – the comic has, in its essence, stayed true to its foundational metaphor.

Over the years, however, the boundaries of this metaphor have gradually thinned and even taken on significantly different characteristics. Perhaps the epitome of this inevitable change is the character of Cyclops, who evolves from a young and optimistic idealist under Xavier's mentorship to a cynical leader who becomes increasingly hardened and obsessed with the survival of his species, seeking to provide them refuge by any means necessary. The zenith of this narrative arc likely occurs with the advent of the so-called Postmodern Comic's Age.[42] In the case of the X-Men series, it reaches its peak with Jonathan Hickman's saga, which began in 2017 and was recently concluded by Gerry Duggan.

A talented writer of the present generation, Hickman lays the foundation for his work in the remarkable run *House of X - Powers of X*, where he skilfully combines four different timelines, completely revolutionising the mutant world. By harnessing the long-hidden powers of Moira MacTaggert, the X-Men discover that all possible futures lead to the inevitable and tragic extinction of their species. The mutants' last remaining hope lies in constructing an independent nation on the sentient island of Krakoa to defend themselves against *Homo sapiens*. The X-Men decide to cease using their powers

42 A. Collerton, 'The Aluminum Age: Postmodern Themes in American Comics Circa 2001–2018', *Thesis*, Georgia State University, Atlanta, 2020, https://doi.org/10.57709/17466605.

to protect a world that fears them and instead use their abilities to assert and safeguard their own identity. The dream of peaceful coexistence with humans has ended. As Xavier reminds the mutants of Krakoa, 'while you slept, the world *changed*' because 'you must see by now there is no you and I, there is only *us*. We are together, or we are nothing'.[43]

Despite their concision, Xavier's words effectively describe the process of postmodern psychological fragmentation of identity politics. This refers to the spread of

> a wide range of political activity founded in the shared experiences lived by the members of certain social groups [...] Members of that constituency assert or reclaim ways of understanding their distinctiveness that challenge dominant characterizations, with the goal of greater self-determination.[44]

As Charles Taylor has argued, 'in the earlier age recognition never arose as a problem' because 'general recognition was built into the socially derived identity by virtue of the very fact that it was based on social categories that everyone took for granted'. Nowadays, the recognition of people's identities is more closely related to the individual perception of it, and 'personal, original identity doesn't enjoy this recognition a priori' but 'it has to win it through exchange, and the attempt can fail'.[45] Moreover, the postmodern concept of identity is characterised by an emphasis on its inner voice and capacity for authenticity – that is, its ability to determine a way of being that is somehow true to oneself. The postmodern attempt to bring together the struggle for recognition of authenticity with the universal claim of liberty and equality could be summarised in the following postmodern motto: be yourself, and reclaim your identity in the public space, marking your difference from others. This process profoundly altered the psychological and sociological mechanisms of integration of others in society, and dramatically changes the very idea of equality as inclusion within a broader political context, with paradoxical effects for postmodern constitutionalism. After having originated to enforce equality between people, the nondiscrimination principle is now used by identity politics to heighten civil and political disagreement.

Hickman's run is deeply influenced by this process. While in the past, the X-Men fought for public recognition of their shared diversity in the name of their individual humanity, today the sole justification of their existence as

43 *X Men: House of X – Power of X* by J. Hickman, 2021.

44 C. Heyes, 'Identity Politics' *Stanford Encyclopedia of Philosophy*, 2016, http://plato.stanford.edu.

45 C. Taylor, 'The Politics of Recognition', in *Multiculturalism: Examining the Politics of Recognition*, ed. A. Gutmann (Princeton: Princeton University Press, 1994): 35–55.

individuals is what sets them apart as different. In other words, identity politics overshadows Xavier's dream of Integrated X-Men, and the comic book portrays a minority that is less willing to integrate because they are increasingly proud of their own diversity.[46] Otherness is no longer synonymous with complexity but with identity assertion.

Hickman's mutant revolution brings about several legal consequences. From a constitutional standpoint, the creation of an independent State somehow mirroring the strategy of current nationalistic populisms, which utilise identity claims to assert their independence and strengthen their sovereignty.[47] The founding of Krakoa Nation is accompanied by the creation of a language that can only be learnt by mutants. This language is developed as part of the process of claiming a 'sentient' territory that has the ability to recognise the genomes of its inhabitants. In this way, Hickman unconsciously re-proposes the Herderian Romantic trinity *Ein Volk, ein Land, eine Sprache*, reproducing the immediate and spontaneous sense of belonging of several individuals to a homogeneous community.

With Great Power Comes Great Revenge? Identity Politics in the X-Men's Green Arc

Hickman's run was concluded by Gerry Duggan, who wrote about the fall of Krakoa and consequently the end of the mutant nationalist dream. However, within the saga, some authors delved deeper into identity politics, even challenging foundational Marvel Universe principles, such as the timeless belief that with great power comes great responsibility.

This focus on identity politics is particularly prominent in Duggan's X-Men Green Arc. The plot is straightforward yet impactful; it introduces Lin Li, also known as Nature Girl, a quiet teenager deeply connected to animals and the natural world. The story begins with an emotional incident – a sea turtle washes ashore on Krakoa, exhausted and entangled in a plastic bag coming from a grocery store in Las Vegas. Though Nature Girl tries to help, the turtle ultimately dies, serving as a catalyst for the narrative.

Profoundly affected by the tragedy, Nature Girl begins to prioritise nature and animals over humans who harm the environment. Using one of Krakoa's

46 See M.J. Theriault, 'For Now, Identity Politics Overshadows Xavier's Dream Of Integrated X-Men', 25 July 2017, https://thefederalist.com/2017/07/25/now-identity-politics-overshadows-xaviers-dream-integrated-x-men/.

47 See L. P. Vanoni and B. Vimercati, 'Identity Politics and Constitutional Disagreement: The Rise of the "New" Populisms and Nationalisms in the Fragmented European Landscape', *Eurojus*, 2/2021, 44–65.

gates, she travels to Las Vegas to confront the manager of the grocery store. After a brief confrontation, she takes matters into her own hands, fatally slitting his throat with a pair of scissors – a shocking act that sets the tone for the storyline. This event sparks a relentless quest for vengeance, leading Nature Girl to confront – and ultimately kill – not only the owners of large corporations but also blue-collar workers on an oil platform. Eventually, Lin is confronted by Xavier, Magneto and the other leaders of the Krakoan Nation. They condemn her actions and, as punishment, banish her to a secluded cave on Krakoa. Nonetheless, the living island of Krakoa itself chooses to forgive her actions and sets her free. Before departing the island, Lin states defiantly:

> I regret lashing out in Las Vegas, but that's where my remorse ends. You [X-Men] taught me to stand up and fight for what I know is right [...] and my cause is right. My anger is just.[48]

The X-Men Green arc is reshaping Marvel's – and, more broadly, the comic book's – philosophy for at least two significant reasons. First, by justifying Nature Girl's anger and actions on the grounds that her cause is noble, the narrative simplifies her character arc and diminishes the inner moral conflict that has long been a cornerstone of the hero's journey. Traditional storytelling has relied heavily on this framework, which is foundational to many of the most cherished classic tales.[49]

This approach examines the concept of personal transformation and growth through both physical and emotional challenges, portraying characters who undergo rites of passage, search for a sense of belonging, and strive to uncover their authentic selves. It reflects the mythic structure of a protagonist's journey, where overcoming obstacles is not just about achieving a goal but also about self-discovery and moral evolution. By sidestepping this complexity, the X-Men Green arc diverges from a long-standing tradition that defines much of what makes heroic storytelling universally resonant. In other words, the X-Men run transforms the hero into a justified victim and – through her actions – into a terrorist, effectively blurring the lines between right and wrong. This moral ambiguity erodes the traditional notions of super-heroism, presenting a protagonist whose decisions are driven by hate and anger and calling into question the very ethics of her crusade.[50] This

48 *X-Men Unlimited – Green* (#1 and 2) by Gerry Duggan, 2022.

49 J. Campbell, *The Hero With a Thousand Faces* (Princeton: Princeton University Press, 2004).

50 For an insightful analysis of Batman's struggle between Law and Justice, see G. Martinico, 'Is Batman Above the Law? Law and Batman Fictional Universe', in *The Law in Graphic Narratives*.

shift in narrative philosophy brings to mind the iconic *Batman: Hush* and the memorable dialogue between Commissioner Gordon and Batman:

> *Gordon*: You and I have seen more than our fair share of tragedies and thirsted for revenge. If Batman wanted to be a killer, he could have started long ago. But, it's a line. On one side we believe in the law. On the other [...] sometimes, the law fails us. Maybe that's why I've understood you [...] allowed you to help protect this city.
> Batman, if you cross that line – if you kill The Joker tonight – I will lead the hunt to bring you to justice. In the eyes of the law [...] in my eyes you'll be no different from him.[51]

Second, and more notably, the X-Men Green arc is redefining the original use of politics in storytelling. According to Stan Lee, Marvel has always been [...] a reflection of the world right outside our window, emphasising that great art – including not just fine art but also commercial art, such as comics – serves as a lens through which we view social and political realities. However, as he stated in a TV interview for AMC in 2017,

> I've always tried to do our stories so that it didn't matter if you were of the white race, the black race, the brown race, or whatever. [...] I tried to incorporate social issues in the background or under laying the plot. But never to the point of letting it interfere with the story or hitting the reader over the head.[52]

The rise of identity politics and the advent of the Comic's Postmodern Age have shifted this narrative dynamic, prioritising social and political issues over the personal conflicts of the characters. This approach often flattens their narrative arcs, reducing the depth and complexity traditionally explored through their individual journeys and inner struggles. As noted by Matthew Theriault:

Legal Perspectives on Comics, Manga and Anime, eds. G. Martinico and G. M. Ruotolo (Berlin: De Gruyter, 2024): 49–65.

51 *Batman: Hush* by J. Loeb, 2003.

52 See Robert Kirkman, *Secret History of Comics*. Interview with Stan Lee, AMC 12 November 2017, reported by C. Bradley, 'Stan Lee Was Right About Politics & Social Issues in Comics', 23 February 2022, https://bleedingfool.com/comics/stan-lee-was-right-about-politics-social-issues-in-comics/.

> Whereas in the Modern Age the reader's primary investment was assumed by each publisher to be in an overarching cape opera, the individual heroes mere windows into more wondrous worlds, in the Postmodern Age of Comics heroes are not windows but mirrors, each a reflection of a particular group of readers the publisher is targeting. It is an approach which presumes the purported narcissism of the Millennial generation, that what each reader really wants are stories of himself in the spandex and skivvies. Put another way, the Modern Age had its focus on immersion, the Postmodern on identification.[53]

In sum, Stan Lee's original vision aimed to confront bigotry, hatred and discrimination through characters' conflicts, dilemmas and narrative arcs – not by directly prioritising specific political issues over storyline or victimising one identity over others. The central theme of the X-Men saga is a condemnation of fear and hatred towards the 'Other', regardless of whether one belongs to the majority or the minority. It advocates not merely for representation, but for coexistence and cooperation. Xavier's Dream – shaped by Dr King Jr's vision – calls for judging individuals not by their skin colour or genetic code, but by the content of their character.[54]

Therefore, the empathy mutants created with readers did not stem from mirroring the readers' specific identities but rather from their conflict-driven narrative arcs, which fostered identification through universal themes of struggle and perseverance. For instance, X-Men: *God Loves, Man Kills* is often associated with the discrimination faced by the LGBTQ+ community. This association arose not because characters like Cyclops or Kitty Pryde were explicitly depicted as LGBTQ+, but because their narrative arcs resonated with readers' personal dilemmas, reflecting broader societal struggles. As the comic book writer Fabian Nicieza pointed out:

> 'Mutants' does not equal one specific aspect of societal prejudices, mutants equal ALL prejudice. Be it race, creed, gender, culture, nationality, sexual orientation, the notion of being feared or despised simply because you are 'different' is not owned by any one segment of the population, but rather, ironically, owned by all of us at one time or another in our lives, and that is why the X-books always flourished after their relaunch, because nearly all readers could empathize with their plight. Even if the 'tragedy' you empathized with was because during your teen years you had a lot of acne, it didn't diminish

53 M. J. Theriault, 'We're Living in the Postmodern Age of Comics', *Hub City Review*, 10 March 2016, https://hubcityreview.com/2016/03/10/were-living-in-the-postmodern-age-of-comics/.
54 M. J. Theriault (see note 46).

> the fact that you still understood what it meant to feel 'different'. Of course, people see things through their own eyes, their own experiences, their own pains, and therefore subscribe their own specific interpretations on their entertainment, usually angling it towards a position that speaks to their own needs, but if you take aerial view rather than a ground level view, you have to realize the concept is an umbrella that covers everything, not just one specific societal group.[55]

Conclusion

As demonstrated in the previous pages, comic books have always been deeply intertwined with politics, as art itself is inherently political, serving as a window into reality. The X-Men comic books are no exception; throughout their long-standing saga, they have tackled themes of prejudice, hatred and bigotry. However, over time, the role attributed to politics within these stories has evolved, altering the delicate balance between social issues and storytelling. This shift has ultimately transformed the very core of superhero philosophy, redefining how these narratives engage with their audiences. The comic book industry has traditionally prioritised storytelling over politics, focussing on crafting compelling character arcs and building strong empathy with readers. Heroes were designed to represent all forms of prejudice, making their struggles universally relatable and allowing readers from diverse backgrounds to connect with their journeys.

The rise of identity politics somehow altered this balance, emphasising the alignment between the reader's identity and the character's traits, ultimately prioritising the victimization of certain identity groups over others. This sometimes amplifies political messaging at the expense of the storyline, transforming superheroes into social justice warriors. However, superheroes were never originally conceived as social justice warriors. Contrary to what DeConnick suggests, Captain America has always stood for liberty and justice – and, especially in times of destruction and turmoil, for the *unity* of all people, transcending divisions rather than reinforcing them.[56]

55 Reported by J. J. Darowski (see note 12).

56 See, for instance, *Ultimate Comics The Ultimates #16* – United We Stand by L. Ross, 2012. The United States of America is falling apart and Captain America, becoming president, stated: 'America is deep in crisis – we're divided, mistrustful, nervous, and scared. America has asked me to lead them. I ask America to look within themselves. My grandmother always said, ask not for challenges equal to our strengths, but for strength equal to our challenges [...] I look at America right now, broken, in pieces, and I remember – I once risked everything to answer a call. I realize now I can do more to serve my country. I know I can do more to live up to my potential.

Concluding her interview, Kelly Sue DeConnick responded to the upset fandom with the statement: 'If you don't like my politics, don't buy my books!'.[57] This remark arguably clashes with the very purpose of the comic book industry, which is to entertain fans who purchase and support comic books. Furthermore, the use of identity politics in comics may directly overshadow the spirit of the Preamble to the famous Marvel Reader's Bill of Rights, signed by Stan Lee himself for Marvel's 30th anniversary:

> All Marvelites are created equal. Your Bullpen will never favor one group of readers over another. Therefore, each and every one of you is irrevocably granted these inalienable rights: [...]'[58]

Once again, the issue does not stem from the presence of politics in comics, but from political messages overcoming the storytelling itself. As Lee and Claremont clearly demonstrated in their runs, the true power of storytelling lies in its ability to reflect universal experiences of prejudice and injustice, enabling readers to see themselves in the characters' journeys, regardless of their specific identity.

This crisis calls us all to do our best. To rebuild our fragile unity. To find strength equal to our challenges. I have decided to answer the call of the people. I accept. I, Steve Rogers – Captain America – Do solemnly swear that I will faithfully execute the Office of the President of the United States. And will, to the best of my ability, preserve, protect, and defend the Constitution of the United States'. See also W. Peitz, 'Captain America: The Epitome of American Values and Identity', Senior Capstone Theses. 6, 2013, https://scholarworks.arcadia.edu/senior_theses/6.

57 K. S. DeConnick (see note 1).

58 The *Marvel Reader's Bill of Rights* was published in the *Soapbox* of Punisher war zone #13, 1992. It is available at http://www.echoesofthemultiverse.com/viewtopic.php?t=1195.

Chapter 5

REFERENCES TO INTERNATIONAL LAW IN HARRY POTTER'S WIZARDING WORLD

Angela Maria Gallo

'Institutional' Profiles of International Law in the *Harry Potter* Saga and *Fantastic Beasts and Where to Find Them*

The magical universe in which J. K. Rowling's novels are set, the Wizarding World, is full of references to magical law and the consequences of its violations.[1]

The legal element represents a relevant aspect both in the *Harry Potter* saga and in *Fantastic Beasts and Where to Find Them*, and contemplates a series of references to institutions of both the domestic and international legal systems, which the author exploits to define as realistically as possible the context in which the story is set.

The Wizarding World is built in a similar way to the real one:[2] within it, for example, the reconstruction of the State apparatus is entirely defined, and

1 In this chapter, there is more reference to the books written by Rowling and less to the films, which often, for cinematographic needs, do not report in great detail the exciting descriptions of the Wizarding World as conceived by the author. On the other hand, to have a more complete picture of the Wizarding World of Harry Potter, we believe it is necessary to also refer to other books written later by Rowling to expand the implications of the narrative and clarify the context in which the narrated events are placed, as well as to the official sites where Rowling dispels doubts and curiosities of the fans.

2 For a reconstruction of the parallels between the English Muggle and magical legal systems, see C. Birch, 'The Chosen One(s): Ethnic Election and Contemporary English National Identity in J. K. Rowling's Harry Potter Series', in *Cultural Politics in Harry Potter: Life, Death and the Politics of Fear*, eds. R. Jarazo-Alvarez and P. Alderete-Diez (New York: Routledge, 2020): 5 ff..; J. E. Thomas, J. Charles Smith, D. Wright, and B. H. Barton, 'Harry Potter and the Law', www.scholarship.law.tamu.edu/facscholar/361.

the perception of the division of powers, at least of the executive and judicial ones, is widely visible.

The same happens for the structure of the international community, understood as a set of States that cooperate to achieve the global security of the Wizarding World. It is precisely on this last aspect that, in the following pages, we will focus our attention.

According to the narrative, in 1692, the representatives of the magical communities from all over the world met in France to approve, within the International Confederation of Wizards (ICW), the International Statute for Magical Secrecy. This international treaty, a cornerstone of the magical world, sanctioned the obligation to hide it from non-wizards, the so-called 'Muggles', to prevent them from resuming the hunt for wizards and witches, with disastrous consequences.

The ICW is inspired by the General Assembly of the United Nations,[3] albeit with some differences dictated by the need to make the narrative simpler and more effective: it is composed of representatives of the governments of all the magical communities of the world, has the task of maintaining peace and security in the magical world and is presided over by a Supreme *Mugwump*, who coordinates its work.[4]

Interestingly, according to what was reported in the first draft of Harry Potter and the Prisoner of Azkaban, this International Magical Organization was initially supposed to take on the structure of a Federation.[5] It was not a Confederation, as Rowling's original idea was to create a single magical State divided into regions with their central administration in the United

---

3 This was confirmed by Rowling herself in a tweet on 8 August 2015. The author usually answers the curiosities of the fans on her Twitter page. For further information, see V. Ndior, 'Relations Internationales and International Law in the Wizarding World', in *Le Droit dans la saga Harry Potter*, eds. V. Ndior and N. Rousseau (Paris: Enrick B Éditions, 2019): 39.

4 We know that Albus Dumbledore, Headmaster of Hogwarts School, was first a delegate representative at the ICW and then Supreme Mugwump, a position from which he was dismissed as soon as he stated at a summit that Voldemort had returned.

5 It should be clarified that by the term 'Confederation' J. K. Rowling intended to evoke the idea that, within the ICW, the States retain their autonomy, as is evident in the saga of *Fantastic Beasts and Where to Find Them* about the history of the Magical Congress of the United States of America (MACUSA). Although the term is misused, it must be admitted that recalling in the name of the ICW the structure of a Confederation makes it immediately clear to the reader that it is a union of States in which each Member has equal weight and value and can participate in the adoption of rules and decisions. In our view, the choice to represent the structure of the ICW in this way is part of the way legal traditions are represented in pop culture to be immediately understandable to the reader. On this aspect, A. Ligustro, R. Tarchi, G. M. Ruotolo, and G. Martinico, *La rappresentazione delle tradizioni giuridiche nella pop culture* (Napoli: Editoriale Scientifica, 2023).

Kingdom. Subsequently, to make the reconstruction of the Wizarding World proposed to readers more convincing, the author decided to transform the regions into States and change the organisation's name from 'International Federation of Sorcerers' to 'International Confederation of Wizards'.

However, in some passages of the saga, Rowling's basic idea influences the narrative to such an extent that it gives the impression that Great Britain is the only member State of the ICW with decision-making powers and that its decisions extend to the other.[6] In our opinion, the fact that some Muggle States are represented as regions in the Wizarding World is also synonymous with a legacy that is not entirely outdated.[7]

The ICW's function as a normative producer is also evident. Still, because of their binding nature, it adopts acts more reminiscent of the Security Council resolutions (particularly those adopted under art. 41 of Chapter VII of the Charter of the United Nations) than the General Assembly recommendations.

The ICW, like the UN, also sets up *Task Forces*, a sort of commission of inquiry with the task of monitoring situations that could, even if only potentially, jeopardise international peace and magical security.[8]

In *Fantastic Beasts and Where to Find Them*, two international Task Forces are mentioned: the permanent Tibet Task Force to monitor the numerous sightings of Yetis by Muggles and the one to eliminate 'illegal wizards'. These are used in the Wizarding World as a prerequisite for outlining interventions in the field of the *Aurors*, that is, members of State law enforcement agencies who have to pass a difficult and highly qualifying training period, following which they can be chosen not only to operate on national territory but also as members of international military operations. In Harry Potter and the Order of the Phoenix, Professor McGonagall explains to Harry Potter that, to become an Auror:

> They ask for a minimum of five NEWTs, and nothing under 'Exceeds Expectations' grade, I see. Then you would be required to undergo a stringent

6 An example is the cataloguing of magical creatures, which we will discuss later. The English Ministry of Magic adopted this practice but later extended it to all other States.

7 In *Fantastic Beasts and Where to Find Them*, Rowling writes about Graphorns (beasts that resemble Muggle bulls): 'The Graphorn is found in mountainous European regions. Large and greyish-purple with a humped back, the Graphorn has two very long, sharp horns, walks on large, four-thumbed feet, and has an extremely aggressive nature'.

8 The plot of the video game Harry Potter: Wizards Unite, developed by Niantic and WB Games San Francisco for Pottermore, is also based on the Ministry of Magic's recruitment of wizards and witches to create a Task Force of the Statute of Secrecy capable of containing the effects produced by the exposure of magic to Muggles.

> series of character and aptitude tests at the Auror office. It's a difficult career path, Potter, they onlytake the best. In fact, I don't think anybody has been taken on in the last three years.[9]

These forces fight the use of dark magic and protect the magical population from those who use it, which shows a substantial similarity to peacekeeping operations. For example, the *Task Force* in Tibet was established by the ICW due to the inability of the magical government to contain and remedy sightings of the Yeti by non-wizards. However, unlike *peacekeeping* operations, which require the consent of the territorial sovereign for their deployment, the operations of the *Aurors* appear more like sanctions, presupposing the will of the ICW to censure the magical governments that have violated, with their behaviour, the Statute of Magical Secrecy as well as to replace them to restore peace and security in their territory.

But the ICW censures magical governments not only when there is a threat to magical peace and security but also when States adopt policies contrary to the principles that underpin the organization, as in the case of the British minister of magic Damocles Rowle,[10] who was forced to resign after receiving censure from the ICW for his anti-Muggle policies and the creation of Azkaban Prison, a Dementor-infested fortress previously used by the dark wizard Ekrizdis in the fifteenth century as his hideout. Minister Rowle's resignation suggests that the ICW's pronouncements and decisions carry so much political weight in the Wizarding World that they also influence the domestic politics of States, and that the ICW, like the UN, has cardinal principles that all members must respect.

'Normative' Profiles of International Law in the Wizarding World

The narrative of the international law elements in the Wizarding World does not stop at the structure of the ICW. Instead, it continues with the provision

---

9 The NEWTs, or Nastily Exhausting Wizarding Tests, are optional exams that Hogwarts students can only take in the seventh year if they have obtained excellent marks in the compulsory exams. They represent a sort of path of excellence for deserving wizards.

10 The name of the minister is evocative of the Greek myth of Damocles, who proved for a day the power and responsibilities of Dionysius, tyrant of Syracuse. The minister's choice to use Azkaban as a maximum-security prison was contested by many wizards and witches because the surveillance of dementors was considered extremely excessive since their presence could instil, even in the quietest prisoners, madness and dangerousness. For further information, see J. K. Rowling, *Hogwarts Tales: Power, Politics, and Poltergeist* (London: Pottermore, 2016): 22.

of some basic principles of the international magical order, also understood as general international law, whose respect cannot be ignored.

In this respect, regarding the procedure of forming customary norms, the Wizarding World is close to the now-outdated consensual doctrine,[11] according to which the consensus of States would also be relevant in forming international customs.

Infact, in the book *Fantastic Beasts and Where to Find Them* there is a discussion that arose within the work of the Magic Council about the cataloguing of magical creatures, during which the Head of the Magic Council, Burdock Muldoon, tried to outline a definition of both magical beings and magical beasts to classify all existing magical creatures and distinguish those with rights and duties (beings) from those who only have rights (beasts), as they are not endowed with intelligence and are therefore unable to comply with the obligations imposed by law. However, the definition provided by Muldoon was unclear and inexhaustive, as he recognized magical beings as 'any member of the magical community that walked on two legs'. In this way, many dangerous magical creatures or those of low intelligence fell within the definition of beings. In contrast, all those quadruped creatures with intelligence were excluded. Muldoon's successors could not do better, and magical creatures had to wait until 1811 to obtain a more transparent and inclusive definition of magical beings. Rowling writes precisely about what has just been stated:

> Not until 1811 were definitions found that most of the magical community found acceptable.[12]

The reference to the agreement of the magical community makes us reflect on how, in the Wizarding World of Harry Potter, the consensus of States represents a constitutive element for the birth of an international magical custom. Only after the States agreed on the meaning of magical beings and magical beasts were international standards adopted regarding the classification of all known beasts and beings, subsequently implemented internally.

Instead, with regard to the material content of the rules of general international law and fundamental principles that characterise the magical community and must be respected, it is interesting to note that the so-called *unforgivable curses* have as their object behaviours prohibited by rules that resemble *jus cogens norms* of international law.

---

11 S. Marchisio, *Corso di diritto internazionale* (Milano: Giappichelli Editore, 2021): 48.

12 J. K. Rowling, *Fantastic Beasts and Where to Find Them* (London: Bloomsbury, 2017): 32.

The prohibition of torture could be transposed into the prohibition of pronouncing the curse *Cruciatus*, which would inflict such acute pain on those who suffer it that it would drive them to madness; the ban on enslavement could instead be transposed into the prohibition of pronouncing the *Imperius* curse, with which a wizard would keep another under his total control to make him act according to his will; and finally, some of the prohibitions of committing crimes against humanity would be transposed into the prohibition of pronouncing the *Avada Kedavra* curse, which would cause the instant death of any living being, be it magical or Muggle.

Unfortunately, as also happens in our Muggle world, these prohibitions are not always respected; unforgivable curses are sometimes used by witches and wizards to kill, control or inflict pain on others without suffering the consequences. Harry Potter himself, following the murder of his godfather Sirius Black by Bellatrix Lestrange, will pronounce the Cruciatus curse to punish the witch.

In addition, the presence of *jus cogens* in the Harry Potter saga is also strengthened by applying the principle of self-determination of peoples to the case of the Centaurs.

The latter proposed an application to the Ministry of Magic to be catalogued as beasts and not as magical beings to conduct their business separately from magicians. If they had been classified as magical beings, they would have had to participate in adopting and respecting magical laws. Still, since Centaurs are distrustful of wizards and possess entirely different cultures and traditions, their contribution would have compromised their cultural identity.[13]

Therefore, the magical community decided to grant the Centaurs permission to live outside society, cataloguing them as magical beasts that do not need protection to hide their magical character from Muggles.

By what has been stated, the magical State authorities created protected forest areas where the Centaurs live undisturbed. Centaurs have been catalogued as XXXX,[14] a category in which aggressive beasts are usually

13 In J. K. Rowling's *Harry Potter and the and the Philosopher's Stone*, (London, Bloomsbury 1997): 250, Rubeus Hagrid, about the Centaurs, says: 'Never', said Hagrid irritably, 'try an' get a straight answer out of a centaur. Ruddy star-gazers. Not interested in anythin' closer'n the moon'. This phrase indicates how far the Centaurs' customs and traditions are from those of the wizards.

14 In *Fantastic Beasts and Where to Find Them*, it is possible to learn how the British Ministry of Magic catalogues beasts (but we know that the other States of the international magical community also follow this approach). According to this cataloguing, beasts classified as XXXXX are considered to kill wizards, and therefore, impossible to train or domesticate; XXXX ones, on the other hand, are considered dangerous and can, thus, only be tackled only by those with

included; however, in this context, the classification aims to warn wizards about the treatment to be reserved for Centaurs, to whom the utmost respect must be given.

This brief explanation of the centaur people provided by the author recalls the category of Indigenous peoples, who have been recognised with the right to self-determination, by which they freely decide their political status and pursue their own economic, social and cultural development, as contemplated by art. 3 of the United Nations Declaration on the Rights of Indigenous Peoples.

Finally, still on the material content of the rules of international law, it is worth analysing the rules for protecting magical creatures in the magical international legal order.

In fact, in the first episode of the *Fantastic Beasts and Where to Find Them* saga, Rowling presents us with a parallel magical world, that of Newt Scamander, a magizoologist who decides to dedicate his life to the care and breeding of magical creatures, especially those in danger of extinction.

In the Scamandrian universe, magical creatures are seen as beings worthy of protection as they cannot hide their magical character; for this reason, art. 73 of the International Code of Magical Secrecy attributes to 'any national administration having authority over magicians' responsibility for acts carried out by a magical creature to the detriment of a Muggle or capable of attracting his attention and establishes sanctions in reaction to the event, which the International Confederation of Magicians will decide.

The magical international (legal) order, in short, seems to recover both the principle of the protection of minorities and the idea of the responsibility of State organs for illegitimate acts carried out by individuals.

A testimony of the existence of the responsibility of States for acts carried out by magical beasts comes from the book *Fantastic Beasts and Where to Find Them*, in which Newt Scamander tells of two cases in which the ICW had to fine Tibet and Scotland for the repeated violation of art. 73. In particular, he states:

> It would be idle to deny that there have been occasional breaches of Clause 73 since it was first put in place. Older British readers will remember the Ilfracombe Incident of 1932, when a rogue Welsh Green dragon swooped down upon a crowded beach full of sunbathing Muggles. Fatalities were

---

specialised knowledge; while the beasts classified as XXX, XX and X do not cause particular problems. Rubeus Hagrid, in chapter 15 of Harry Potter and the Philosopher's Stone, explains to Harry Potter that: 'They're deep, mind, centaurs [...] they know things [...] jus' don' let on much'.

> mercifully prevented by the brave actions of a holidaying wizarding family (subsequently awarded Orders of Merlin, First Class), when they immediately performed the largest batch of Memory Charms this century on the inhabitants of Ilfracombe, thus narrowly averting catastrophe.

However, the magizoologist, precisely to underline the consequences of the offense, recalls in a note that:

> In his 1972 book *Muggles Who Notice*, Blenheim Stalk asserts that some residents of Ilfracombe escaped the Mass Memory Charm. 'To this day, a Muggle bearing the nickname "Dodgy Dirk" holds forth in bars along the south coast on the subject of a "dirty great flying lizard" that punctured his lilo"'.

Harry Potter and International Trade

Also, the issue of international magical trade is relevant to the Harry Potter saga. Scrolling through the pages of the seven books that make up the Harry Potter saga, it seems that serious business is involved in the Wizarding World. It has given rise to an Office of the British Ministry of Magic for cooperation in international magical trade. The first time reference is made to this cooperation is in *Harry Potter and the Goblet of Fire*, when a character, Percy Weasley (one of Ron's brothers), states that he is working on a report for the Department of International Magical Cooperation on the subject of cauldrons and adds that the study will serve to establish international standards for the thickness of the bottoms of cauldrons. Subsequently, in a descriptive sequence in which we see Harry preparing to face the hearing for violating the prohibition of the use of magic for minors outside the walls of Hogwarts, the elevator of the Ministry of Magic necessary to reach the Court[15] stops at the fifth level and announces:

> Level Five, Department of International Magical Cooperation, incorporating the International Magical Trading Standards Body, the International Magical Office of Law and the International Confederation of Wizards, British Seats.[16]

15 The court that judges Harry Potter for violating the ban, which applies to minors, on the use of magic in the Muggle world, is called the Wizengamot, whose seat is located on the basement floor of the Ministry of Magic building. Symbolic, in our view, is the choice to locate the Ministry of Magic and the Wizengamot (which serves as both the Supreme Court and Parliament) in the same building, as if to concentrate all State power in one place.

16 J. K. Rowling, *Harry Potter and the Order of the Phoenix* (London: Bloomsbury, 1997): 120.

These are the English headquarters of an International Magical Trading Standards Organization, responsible for supervising the customs and commercial practices established in the Wizarding World and proposing trade agreements relating to the trade of goods and services inspired by the principles of cooperation and liberalisation of international trade. This organisation, at least in terms of its functions, is reminiscent of the Muggle World Trade Organization (WTO), which has been responsible for regulating international trade relations since 1995.[17]

We also know that there is a classification of tradable and non-marketable goods that emanates from the British Office for International Magical Cooperation, which divides goods into class A marketable and non-marketable materials, and class B marketable and non-marketable materials, depending on the degree of danger they present.

In this regard, Newt Scamander, in his bestseller *Fantastic Beasts and Where to Find Them*,[18] speaking of the Romanian Longhorn and the Erumpent (two magical creatures), points out that the horn and tail of the two beasts are classified as dangerous and subject to strict controls. For this reason, they have been given class B of marketable materials.[19]

Since, as illustrated in *Harry Potter and the Order of the Phoenix*, it is implied that the Department of International Magical Cooperation is also responsible for transposing international trade regulations, we hypothesise that this classification is also the result of agreements concluded by States to regulate international trade relations.

Finally, regarding the existence of an apparatus of international rules relating to global trade, it is helpful to remember the story of Norbert, a dragon belonging to the Norwegian Ridgeback family, whom Hagrid had raised in his house and whose existence Ron, Hermione and Harry, the protagonists of the saga, learn about by chance.

In the chapter narrating this story, Ron exclaims loudly:

> Dragon-breeding was outlawed by the Warlocks' Convention of 1709, everyone knows that. It's hard to stop Muggles noticing us if we're keeping dragons

---

17 For further information, see P. Picone and L. Ligustro, *Diritto dell'Organizzazione mondiale del commercio* (Padova: Cedam, 2002): 3 ss.

18 Rowling writes this book using literary fiction. Playing on the figure of Newt Scamander, a well-established magizoologist in the Wizarding World, she attributes to him the writing of Fantastic Beasts and Where to Find Them, which later become the textbook for first-year students of Hogwarts School of Wizardry.

19 J. K. Rowling, *Fantastic*, 22–24.

in the back garden – anyway, you can't tame dragons, it's dangerous. You should see the burns Charlie's got off wild ones in Romania.[20]

We have no other information about this Convention, which is always designed to hide the Wizarding World from Muggles. However, we note a certain similarity with the Convention on International Trade in Endangered Species of Wild Fauna and Flora of 1979, although the latter was adopted to protect endangered flora and fauna.

International Cooperation in Harry Potter and Fantastic Beasts

In addition to cooperation between States in international trade, sports are another area in which States are committed to cooperating globally.[21]

In fact, in the Wizarding World of Harry Potter, Quidditch is undoubtedly the most internationally followed sport, to the point that, in *Harry Potter and the Goblet of Fire*, Barty Crouch, the director of the British Office for International Magical Cooperation, declares that he had to organise Portkeys[22] on five continents to allow all those who follow this sport to go to the Quidditch World Cup.[23]

The very fact that the director of the British Office for International Magical Cooperation has obtained permission from other States to install portkeys on their continents is an indication of genuine cooperation between States in the field of sport, which becomes evident in the book *Quidditch Beyond the Ages*, in which the existence of an *International Confederation of the Quidditch* Magic Committee is reported, an agency of the ICW with the task of regulating Quidditch at the international level.

20 J. K. Rowling, *Harry Potter and the Philosopher's Stone*, (London: Bloomsbury, 1998): 169.

21 For further information on the law of sport in the Harry Potter saga, see R. Maurer, 'Le droit du sport et les competitions sportives', in Le *Droit dans la saga Harry Potter*, eds. V. Ndior and N. Rousseau (Paris: Enrick B Éditions 2019): 39.

22 It is one of the means of locomotion that wizards use to teleport from one place to another without being noticed by Muggles. It consists of a bewitched object, which, when touched, transports a wizard to a predetermined place.

23 The scene described by Rowling is that of a conversation between Barty Crouch and Ludo Bagman in which the latter asks the former: 'So, been keeping busy, Barty?' and Director Crouch replies: 'Fairly [...] Organising Portkeys across five continents is no mean feat, Ludo'. In addition, there is an undeniable correlation between the Quidditch World Cup and the Muggle World Cup. Both tournaments are played every four years and provide for the delivery of a cup to the winning team.

In addition to promoting Quidditch worldwide, the Confederation monitors compliance with international magical security by States, which must adopt anti-Muggle measures to avoid exposing the Wizarding World to the danger of being discovered by the no-mags.

In this regard, the Statute of Magical Secrecy of 1962 established the responsibility of each minister of magic for the consequences of magical sports played in their territories.[24] This rule led to the internal establishment of State bodies responsible for regulating magical safety in sports, just as happened with the Department for Magical Games and Sports, created by Great Britain to remedy the problem of Quidditch teams playing near places frequented by Muggles.

By the time of the British Quidditch World Cup, which Ron and Harry attended, the entire organisation was already entrusted to the National Departments for Games and Magical Sports (depending on the Country that would host the tournament), which were concerned not only with finding the appropriate place to play the matches but carried out anti-Muggle magic, in compliance with the Statute of Magical Secrecy.

However, international cooperation in the field of sport does not stop at the organisation of the Quidditch World Cup; in fact, it also exists in the organisation of other types of games, such as, for example, the Triwizard Tournament. Well, in the same year that Harry Potter attends the Quidditch World Cup, Great Britain also hosts the Triwizard Tournament at Hogwarts School, where wizards from other States and schools arrive. The game involves overcoming the three wizards chosen by the Goblet of Fire during the selection phase and arduous and dangerous tests specially designed to test the participants' courage, intelligence and skill. Also, in this case, for the safety of wizards and witches, the organisation is delegated to the Department for Magical Games and Sports, which requires the host school to comply with the anti-Muggle measures issued by the Ministry of Magic, in compliance with the Statute of Magical Secrecy.

Finally, traces of international cooperation between magical States can also be found in criminal matters.

An example is the extradition of the powerful dark wizard Gellert Grindelwald by the Magical Congress of the United States of America (MACUSA) to Europe to try him for his crimes. In the film *Fantastic Beasts and Where to Find Them*, Seraphina Picquery, Head of MACUSA, is seen chairing a meeting with a delegation of the ICW in the MACUSA Pentagram Office to discuss the events in New York (i.e. the murder of some Muggles, including

24 J. K. Rowling, *Quidditch Through the Age* (London: Bloomsbury 2002): 20.

that of Senator Henry Shaw Jr), as a result of which it was believed that international magical security had been seriously endangered.

The Confederation insists on intervening but, in the end, leaves the matter to MACUSA, which nevertheless agrees to cooperate with the European States (it is not specified which ones) to have Grindelwald tried before their judges.

In the film *Fantastic Beasts: The Crimes of Grindelwald*, we see the moment of the extradition of the dark wizard, who is transported to Europe by a flying carriage guarded by the Aurors. We do not know if States conclude magical international criminal law treaties with the objective of cooperation in the fight against cross-border crime. However, we recognise that the ICW has an essential role in the matter as an organisation that pursues peace and security in the magical world and, therefore, influences the choices of States regarding the need to cooperate to flush out criminals and punish them appropriately.

Conclusion

In light of what we have said so far, it seems possible to say that the Wizarding World contemplates its version of the international legal order: the author's use of international legal instruments and institutions, as well as principles crystallised in international law, allows us to connote the narration of a *quid plus* able to place the story in a space-time context easily identifiable by readers. In fact, through these references, she better justifies the actions and reactions of her characters and the events that occur in both Newt Scamander and Harry Potter.

In her novels, therefore, the author gives us a common vision of the way international organisations and international law rules operate. Starting from the choice to attribute to the ICW the power to censor governments unable to maintain peace and security within the borders of their territories, the author reflects the vision of the United Nations as an organisation capable of interfering, even with force, in the affairs of individual States. Additionally, unforgivable curses reflect the familiar feeling regarding the commission of severe international offences perpetrated against individuals. Finally, the protection of magical creatures represents the shared vision that people have of the protection of the weakest subjects.

Furthermore, the existence of unforgivable curses, not provided for by the Code of Magical Secrecy but unambiguous and universal for all magical States, as well as the self-determination of the centaur people, is proof of the presence of general international law in the Wizarding World.

The profile of international trade is also entirely outlined, with Rowling having provided for a magical international trade organisation in some ways similar to our International Trade Organization: both pursue the ultimate goal of regulating international trade through the proposal of trade agreements, inspired by the principles of cooperation and liberalisation of global trade.

Finally, the theme of international cooperation returns in a predominant way also with regard to sport and the fight against crime, a necessary discipline to maintain the peace and security of the Wizarding World, as established by the Statute of Magical Secrecy, a treaty of unparalleled importance in the Wizarding World. It is precisely from this Statute that the author derives the birth of the international magical legal system, understood as a set of legally equal sovereign States, similar to how we internationalists view the Peace of Westphalia of 1648.[25]

25 U. Villani, *Lezioni di diritto internazionale* (Bari: Cacucci, 2021): 4.

Chapter 6

DOING INTERNATIONAL LAW WITH EARBUDS: SOME ISSUES IN HEAVY METAL MUSIC

Gianpaolo Maria Ruotolo*

A Methodological Premise

This chapter is part of a broader research project I have been conducting for several years on the modalities in which popular ('pop') culture narrates legal phenomenons, and international law in particular. I begin by examining the ways in which international law is narrated in comic books.[1]

During the last phase of the latter investigation, I somehow realised that some of these modalities show peculiarities with regard to some *extreme* musical genres, which I know as a listener and a fan: I therefore switched to investigating the way international law issues are used in heavy metal music, trying in the meantime to understand if there were any links with the subject of my previous attention, comics.

So, this chapter, after preliminarily highlighting some themes that bring comics and general pop music together (and this in order to help the reader to walk the same thread I have been following), will highlight some of the elements of the relationship between some subgenres of pop music and international law (that will later be useful to trace some peculiarities of heavy metal approaches) and, on this basis, will then proceed to study the specific case of heavy metal with regard to some bands which, due to certain themes and modes of expression, are of particular interest because they explicitly

---

* All websites accessed on 19 November 2024.

1 See G. M. Ruotolo, 'International Superheroes Law', in *The Law in Graphic Narratives: Legal Perspectives on Comics, Manga and Anime*, eds. G. Martinico and G. M. Ruotolo (Berlin/Boston: De Gruyter, 2024): 191.

deal with aspects of the life of States and individuals which are regulated by international law.

From a methodological perspective, I need to point out that, for rather obvious reasons, the first part of the chapter can't use the typical tools of the (international) lawyer. Indeed, it represents, for me, an incursion into an alien territory and is therefore to be benevolently read in a merely descriptive sense, and just as an instrument for what I will say later, when I will try to highlight, with a case study approach, some international law issues and rules in some songs I've chosen in order to try to show *how* this is done.

Furthermore, it must be said that in the context of the scientific and academic analysis of heavy metal music, the so-called heavy metal studies,[2] an analysis of the legal profiles is almost completely absent,[3] since they adopt sociological, psychological, cultural, ethnological or more strictly musicological approaches. With this contribution, I will therefore try to offer some elements to begin to fill this gap, especially from the perspective of international law studies, obviously in an absolutely partial way.

Furthermore, a job like the one I have done and am doing on requires listening to an enormous amount of material that needs to be catalogued. It is impossible, in a context such as this, to describe all the material that has been collected and classified, so I will limit myself to using some pieces of music that seem, to me at least, to be particularly representative of some approaches that certain bands, coming from specific geographical-cultural contexts, have taken to issues related to international law. I hope I will be able to provide a complete report of the material I am cataloguing in the future.

As far as the structure of the work is concerned, after a first part in which I will highlight some links between comics and pop and rock music in general, I will examine the way in which some issues related to international law are dealt with in some non-metal pop music, and then move on to the latter to highlight some differences that characterise it.

---

2 For some examples in different disciplinary perspectives see A. R. Brown and K. Spracklen et al. (eds.), *Global Metal Music and Culture: Current Directions in Metal Studies* (New York/London: Routledge, 2016); G. Bayer (ed.), *Heavy Metal Music in Britain* (Routledge: London/New York, 2009); M. LaVine, *Heavy Metal Islam – Rock, Resistance and the Struggle for the Soul of Islam* (Oakland: University of California Press, 2008); F. Heesch and N. Scott (eds.), *Heavy Metal Gender and Sexuality* (Routledge: London/New York, 2016); N. Varas-Diaz, D. Nevarez Araujo, E. Rivera-Segarra et al. (eds.), *Heavy Metal Music in Latin America: Perspectives from the Distorted South* (New York/London: Lexington, 2020); J. Wallach, H. M. Berger, and P. D. Greene (eds.), *Metal Rules the Globe – Heavy Metal Music around the World* (Durham: Duke University Press, 2011).

3 For an exception, see C. Hiebaum, 'Law and Its Cultural Representations (with a Focus on Heavy Metal Studies)', in *The Law of the Metal Scene – An Interdisciplinary Discussion*, ed. P. Pichler (Stuttgart: Kohlhammer, 2024): 11 ff.

Lastly, I have decided to limit my references here to bands that have had some commercial success, in order to avoid having to study a very large and multifaceted context such as the underground.

The Relationship between Comics and Pop Music: An Introduction by Way of Justification

According to a widespread perception, comics are still placed on a rather low level of that scale – a scale that, frankly, I think is no longer representative of reality and of the quality of some works – that would distinguish high art from low.

The same level is occupied by pop, in its broadest sense, all the music conceived and produced for popular, urban and mass consumption in the era of industrial civilization, and which, as such, has taken the place, in terms of both function and use, of musical folklore, a legacy of agricultural and pastoral civilization, 'from which it inherits certain modes of fruition but not of production, no longer autogenous but delegated to a creativity strongly influenced by new forms of communication'.[4]

It should be noted at once that the latter artistic expression in its general sense has become global, as it is devoid of any regional connotation. From an artistic point of view, it branches out into a plurality of genres and subgenres. Some of these are widely diffused, while others are not widespread among the generality of listeners and find their success among a more specialised audience. It is in the latter sense that we can include in pop music some *niche* musical genres, such as heavy metal,[5] which can be considered pop in a specific cultural context, as it is the object of commercial exploitation and is opposed to the so-called serious music, which implies advanced structural and theoretical considerations (and this in spite of the high-level musical technicality of metal) and that can be inscribed in a written musical tradition.

What's more, comics and pop music have in common not only their commercial connotations but also the fact that, at least in general and in terms of their origins – which, it should be remembered, do not coincide chronologically – they are both aimed at the same audience: adolescents.

4 www.treccani.it/enciclopedia/pop/. The translation is mine.

5 I am perfectly aware that heavy metal is fragmented into a myriad of subgenres (ranging from the 'A' of 'Alternative metal' to the 'V' of 'Viking metal': https://lambgoat.com/lists/1/the-complete-a-z-of-heavy-metal-subgenres), perhaps more than any other musical genre, and that mainstream metal has to be distinguished from underground metal. But for the objective of this investigation, such a distinction, complex and in any case not univocally shared, is not particularly significant, so I'll speak of heavy metal as a whole.

The first comic strip in the modern sense is traditionally considered to be *The Yellow Kid*, created by the American cartoonist Richard Felton Outcault and published from 1895 in the Sunday supplement of the New York World, while there is a tendency to consider pop born with rock 'n' roll in the fifties (to borrow the words of Muddy Waters in 1977: 'the blues had a baby and they named it rock & roll').

Both deal with themes of youthful rebellion, group cultural identity and the desire for change, if not social subversion. Indeed, both comics and pop music, rock and heavy metal in particular, have often been accused of being forms of escapism, if not outright causes of youthful deviance.

But the link between comics and pop music has always been more explicit than just these suggestions; one could think that one of the greatest American comic book authors, Jack Kirby (1917–1994), was a pioneer in many genres. Although he became famous worldwide mainly for his work in the superhero genre, he also helped popularise romantic comics among the general public, especially through his work for the Marvel publishing house. In November 1971, a comic book was published that presented a teenage love story set during the Woodstock concert, in which the adventures of the protagonists intertwine with the performances of some of the musical stars of that famous event, such as Janis Joplin, Ritchie Havens and Country Joe McDonald[6].

And many other comics published in the United States have music as a key element, used to define the atmosphere and tone of the narrative. For example, to represent a girl who goes wrong and shows a rebellious attitude, she was often depicted dancing (!); one can think of Mary Jane Watson, the wife of Peter Parker, Spider-Man, in her rebellious sixties and seventies phase.[7]

In addition to creating stories with fictional musicians and bands, comics soon began to include real-life pop idols to attract teenage audiences, such as Elvis and the Beatles: in March 1965, for example, issue 130 of *Strange Tales* magazine featured a short story in which The Thing and the Human Torch of the Fantastic Four met the Beatles.

One may also cite *Murder Falcon*, a graphic novel by Johnson Daniel Warren, in which the classic canons of the struggle between good and evil take on the saving form of metal: monstrous beings from another dimension, immune to the power of conventional weapons, suffer only the blows coming from a heavy metal band, whose music is able to evoke warrior spirits capable of fighting and opposing the invaders. Under a kitsch veneer that seems to limit itself to celebrating metal music, the culture and the iconography linked to it in a lavish, exaggerated and tacky way, *Murder Falcon* conveys an important message through its protagonist, a character with a deep and complex personal

6 Issue 14 of the series 'My Love', November 1971.

7 Amazing Spider-Man #47 (by Stan Lee and John Romita).

history marked by illness. Let me also remember *Black Metal* (2007), a series of graphic novels by Rick Spears, that tell the epic story of a pair of brothers with a funereal expression and long, black, flowing hair. The two are, needless to say, black metal fanatics and a caricature of the archetypal metalhead: angry, misanthropic, always dissatisfied and at war with the whole universe.

Moreover, the influence of comics on pop music is twofold, in the sense that not only are comics influenced by music, but many pop musicians use comics or visual forms derived from them to complete their work; one can think, for example, of the collaboration between David Bowie and the cartoonist Mike Allred,[8] or the fact that there are comics that tell the exploits of bands (the very famous case of Kiss, treated as superheroes in the Marvel context), not to mention the case of biographical comics of musicians.

Outside the Anglo-Saxon scenario, but still in the West, in Europe, rock and comics form a sacred and solid alliance. It happened at first in 1974 with the publication of the first issue of the magazine *Metal Hurlant/Heavy Metal*, created by Les Humanoïdes Associés, Jean Giraud and Philippe Druillet.

And even oriental authors have highlighted the passions and influences of music; just think of manga such as *Bastard!!* by Kazushi Hagiwara[9] or *Jojo* by Hirohiko Araki,[10] which are full of quotes and references to the world of rock and metal through the names of the characters that make up the stories, or *Detroit Metal City* by Kiminori Wakasugi,[11] whose protagonist is the frontman of a death metal band (a musical genre that the character himself hates).

And for Italy, we can at least mention the case of *Heavy Bone*, created by the Apulian artist and writer Enzo Rizzi,[12] which tells the adventures of an unleashed anti-hero, a zombie whose first goal is to eliminate all the people who deliberately brought heavy music to earth, which should have been the exclusive prerogative of hell.

So, heavy metal music is often associated with themes of rebellion and protest; indeed, the genre has a long history of opposition to social and cultural norms, and its lyrics often address issues of injustice, oppression and personal freedom. Similarly, comic books, especially those featuring superheroes or antiheroes, often explore the struggle against injustice and the search for freedom. For example, works such as *V for Vendetta* use their narratives to address themes of political oppression and resistance, paralleling the messages of many heavy metal songs.[13]

---

8 M. Allred and S. Horton, *Stardust, Rayguns, & Moonage Daydreams* (San Diego: Insight Comics, 2020).
9 *Basutādo!! Ankoku no hakaishin*, 1988–2010.
10 *Jojo no kimyō na bōken*, 1986-ongoing.
11 *Detoroito Metaru Shiti*, 2005–2010.
12 E. Rizzi, *Heavy Bone* (London: Cut-Up, 2013).
13 A. Moore and D. Lloyd, *V for Vendetta* (New York: DC Comics, 1982–1985).

This synergy between music and comics creates a cultural dialogue that reflects some contemporary social and political concerns at the heart of the international law debate, as we will see.

International Law in Music: Some Examples from Afrobeat, Hip-hop, Alternative and Classic Rock.

Non-experts in both, whether musicians or lawyers, may think that law and music are two very different and distant fields, in the first of which there are binding rules, while in the second creative freedom is the norm.

But apart from the fact that music also has its own rules, which are very complex as anyone who has studied it knows, the relationship between the two is ancient and, as far as international law is concerned, bilateral. In ancient Greece, India, China, pre-Columbian America and pre-colonial Africa, to name but a few, music played a key role in transmitting and disseminating law among citizens, regulating social order, performing judicial functions and even serving as an instrument of dissent to denounce bad government.

Today, due to the increasing irrelevance of borders – and thus the incapacity of domestic law – international law (both public and private) is called upon to regulate transnational cases of musical relevance under innumerable profiles.

What's more, its content can be described and even influenced by music.

In short, we could speak of *international music law* and *international law in music*.

Regarding the first, which I will not deal with here, let me just remind you that international law affects many aspects of music. To mention just a few, think of the freedom of expression that allows creation, plagiarism, the rights of authors, the rights of exploiters and users, especially in the context of the so-called new technologies, antitrust issues related to the relationship between commercial operators and competition, and issues related to live music.

International organisations have recognised the vital role of music from a cultural perspective. In 2011, the General Conference of the United Nations Educational, Scientific and Cultural Organization (UNESCO) proclaimed April 30 as International Jazz Day, emphasising that jazz is a means to develop and increase intercultural exchange and understanding between cultures for the purpose of mutual understanding and tolerance,[14] and inscribed in the Representative List of the Intangible Cultural Heritage of Humanity, in 2018, the reggae music of Jamaica for 'its contribution to the international

14 See UNESCO General Conference, 36th, 2011 [1473], doc. 36 C/Resolutions, para. 39.

discourse on issues of injustice, resistance, love and humanity' and, in 2021, the Congolese rumba for its ability to 'transmit the social and cultural values of the region and to promote intergenerational and social cohesion and solidarity'.

As for *international law in music*, it must be said that the way in which a phenomenon is described in a specific popular context, through a specific popular medium, can tell us a lot about the way in which the same phenomenon is read by the users of that specific medium: indeed, issues of international law are addressed in specific musical contexts, and they often pick up very sensitive themes and issues faced by practitioners and studied by scholars, as I'll try to show.

Moreover, the use of popular media can help describing some phenomena regulated by international law and make them understandable even to those who do not have specific knowledge, thus contributing to the diffusion of legal concepts, whether from a didactic or a more informative perspective. Students will certainly be aided in their understanding of legal dynamics by the use of music they know and love, which may help reduce the gap in knowledge between professors and students.[15]

Moreover, since music deeply touches human beings, it can certainly represent an incentive to reflect on the issues it deals with and, therefore, raise the listener's awareness of these issues.

It is (also) in this sense that I will follow the musical example with a brief description of the international law issues it addresses.

There could be hundreds of examples, in all genres, especially those that use the song form or at least have lyrics. Let me just try to show some non-metal examples with a cherry picking approach,[16] before moving on to the heavy metal context in the next paragraphs.

Fela Kuti (1938–1997) was a famous and very prolific Nigerian musician who, among other things, was the father of Afrobeat, a genre that fuses various expressions of traditional African and African American music such as funk, R&B and highlife. He also became known for his political activism for human rights and political struggles against the Nigerian government.

---

15 In the same sense, see G. Martinico in this volume.

16 Some of the songs I'll deal with in this paragraph can be found in 'TWAILR Mixtape: A playlist for rethinking the spirit and purpose of international law' at https://twailr.com/twailr-mixtape-a-playlist-for-rethinking-the-spirit-and-purpose-of-international-law/. For another analysis of pop songs from an international law perspective, see the page '*En musique: comme un air de droit international…*' of the Centre de Droit International of the Université Libre De Bruxelles, at https://cdi.ulb.ac.be/en-musique-comme-un-air-de-droit-international/.

In 'Beasts of No Nation' (1989), he strongly criticised the right of veto in the United Nations Security Council, calling it 'animal sense':

Dem call the place United Nations
East West Block versus West Block East
No be there dem dey oh United Nations
Disunited United Nations
One veto vote is equal to 92 [...] or more, or more
What kind sense be dat
'Na animal sense

Now, as is well known, Security Council both in its composition and voting techniques, especially art. 27 of the UN Charter,[17] is a very hot issue among international lawyers, be they practitioners or scholars.[18]

Fela's youngest son, Seun Kuti (1983–), as a political activist, promoted a movement 'for African people all over the world to rediscover themselves. To remember that the only thing that unites black people globally, the only thing we all have in common, is that we are from Africa'. As a musician, in 2014, in his song 'IMF', he criticizes the Bretton Woods Institutions for their responsibility towards developing Countries and the entire Global South:

You bring pain
You bring tears
You bring suffering
To my people
International Mother Fucker eh You bring pain
So much lying from the IMF
So much stealing from the IMF
So much killing from the IMF
Manipulation from the IMF
Intimidation from the IMF
Dem and their World Bank brothers

17 '1. Each member of the Security Council shall have one vote. 2. Decisions of the Security Council on procedural matters shall be made by an affirmative vote of nine members. 3. Decisions of the Security Council on all other matters shall be made by an affirmative vote of nine members including the concurring votes of the permanent members; provided that, in decisions under Chapter VI, and under paragraph 3 of Article 52, a party to a dispute shall abstain from voting'.

18 On this issue, from an international law perspective, see B. Fassbender, *UN Security Council Reform and the Right of Veto. A Constitutional Perspective* (Leiden: Brill, 1998) and S. Hassler, *Reforming the UN Security Council Membership* (London: Routledge, 2012); P. Nadin, *UN Security Council Reform* (London: Routledge, 2016).

In international organizations law, the powers, competencies and activities of the IMF and the World Bank are at stake even in the mainstream academic literature: 'interactions with States in the Global South claim that the Fund remains quite captured by the politics of the Washington Consensus, and thus continues to play favorites while promoting or enforcing policies centered on fiscal consolidation on others'.[19]

In 'Here Comes the Judge', Jamaican reggae musician Peter Tosh (1944–1987) imagines a trial in which colonial and imperial States and their actors (Christopher Columbus, Francis Drake, Bartolomé de las Casas, Vasco De Gama, Alexander the Great, John Hannon, James Grant, David Livingstone, John Constantine, Henry Morgan, Marco Polo) are prosecuted for their activities:

> Silence in the court
> The court is in session
> You're all brought here on
> Count one: robbing and raping Africa
> Count two: stealing black people out of Africa
> Count three: brainwashing black people
> Count four: holding black people in captivity for more than 300 years
> Count five: killing over 50 million black people without a cause
> Count six: teaching black people to hate themselves

As well known, the right to self-determination, which was originally provided for exclusively by a treaty provision, in particular by art. 1 of the United Nations Charter, is today a peremptory norm of general international law and one of the cornerstones of the contemporary international legal order. Even if it must be said that it cannot be reduced to a single, self-sufficient norm, it was certainly born in the context of decolonization, in order to recognize the right of every State to decide on its own political status, its own system of government, and to pursue its economic, social and cultural development, without suffering external interference, and, conversely, the obligation of all other States to respect this right. In the words of Antonio Cassese, self-determination was 'perceived and relied upon as a legal right to decolonization'.[20]

---

19 C. Kennedy-Hernandez, in *Oxford Handbook of the International Monetary Fund*, eds. B. Momani and M. Hibben (Oxford: Oxford University Press, 2024): 658.

20 A. Cassese, 'Treaty law' in *Self-Determination of Peoples: A Legal Reappraisal* (Cambridge: Cambridge University Press, 1995): 65.

In 'Living Like a Refugee,' the Refugee All-Stars of Sierra Leone, a band formed by a group of refugees who fled to Guinea during the Sierra Leone Civil War (1991–2002), draw on their life experiences to dramatise the experiences of their peers:

> You left your country to seek refuge
> In another man's land
> You will be confronted by strange dialects
> And you will be fed with unusual diets
> You've got to sleep in a tarpaulin house
> Which is so hot
> You've got to sleep on a tarpaulin mat
> Which is so cold
> Living like a refugee is not easy

General international law does not provide for a subjective right to immigration of individuals; that is to say, it does not in any way oblige States to allow the entry of all aliens into their territory, leaving the regulation of this matter to the competence of the domestic legal system and, in the absence of special protection needs (think, for example, of the need to protect human life at sea), it therefore limits to requiring States to allow the crossing of borders only by their own citizens.

The above-mentioned provisions, which are limited to providing for the right of an individual to leave any Country but to enter it only in the presence of that special link constituted by citizenship, recognize subjective rights of emigration and repatriation, but not a right of immigration, understood as the right to enter any foreign Country with a view to settling there.

In very general terms, moreover, asylum can be defined as temporary or permanent protection granted by a State to an alien who requests it; this protection can be granted either by receiving the alien in one of its diplomatic missions abroad (so-called diplomatic asylum) or by allowing the alien to enter the national territory (so-called territorial asylum).

If, therefore, with regard to the conditions for granting the right of asylum, States appear to be essentially free from general international obligations, it is with regard to the category of refugees that such obligations come to the fore: in this matter the well-known Geneva Convention of 1951 on the Status of Refugees assumes primary importance. Let me recall that art. 1, par. 2 of the Convention grants the status of refugee to those who 'have a well-founded fear of being persecuted for reasons of race, religion, nationality, membership of a particular social group or political opinion, who are outside the Country of their nationality and are unable or unwilling to avail themselves of the protection of that Country'. It is clear from this provision that the Convention requires its Parties to grant refugee status to persons who simultaneously meet three distinct conditions: (a) they have suffered, or are in danger of suffering, persecution for which there is 'serious evidence'; (b) they have been the object of an enforced removal from their Country of nationality; and (c) they are unable to avail themselves of the protection of that Country.

An analogue dramatic context inspired both the title and the lyrics of the 2005 song 'Diamonds from Sierra Leone' by the American rapper Kanye West (1977–), which focusses on one of the key circumstances of a civil war:

> They pray for the death of our dynasty like 'Amen'
> Right here stands a man
> With the power to make a diamond with his bare hands
> Diamonds are forever (forever, forever)
> Throw your diamonds in the sky if you feel the vibe

International law provides for a definition of so-called blood diamonds: according to the United Nations, a blood diamond is any diamond extracted from regions under the control of factions opposed to the legitimate government of a State, sold to finance military operations against that government and to provide weapons and military supplies to the rebels, some of whom have engaged in extremely violent campaigns that have caused considerable suffering to civilian populations. This definition was drafted in the 1990s, a period marked by severe civil conflicts in various parts of West and Central Africa, where rebel groups operated in diamond-rich regions. Three conflicts in particular – in Angola, Democratic Republic of the Congo and Sierra Leone – drew attention to the harmful effects of diamonds, although similar problems existed in other Countries. The Kimberley Process Certification Scheme (KPCS) was established by the United Nations in 2002 to prevent the trade in conflict diamonds and to ensure that diamonds sold on the international market are conflict-free.

This initiative, one of those catalogued by scholars as an expression of so-called informal international lawmaking,[21] was a response to growing concerns about the link between diamonds, human rights abuses and armed

21 The doctrine speaks of informal international lawmaking (IN-LAW) to cover cases of cross-border cooperation between public authorities, which may involve the participation of private and international organizations, and States. J. Pauwelyn, R. A. Wessel, and J. Wouters (eds.), *Informal International Lawmaking* (Oxford: Oxford University Press, 2012); J. Pauwelyn, R. A. Wessel, and J. Wouters, 'When Structures Become Shackles: Stagnation and Dynamics in International Lawmaking', *European Journal of International Law*, 2014 (25): 733.

conflicts, and involves collaboration between governments, the diamond industry and civil society to create a system that would prevent conflict diamonds from entering the global market.

Despite its intentions, the effectiveness of the KPCS has been questioned, with some studies suggesting that it has not adequately addressed the complexities of the diamond trade and the issues related to human rights abuses. What's more, from a legal perspective, the UN definition focuses only on diamonds that finance insurgencies against a government, ignoring or underestimating situations where, as in Zimbabwe, officials of legitimate governments use their authority over legal diamond operations to enrich themselves, maintain their power or benefit their associates, often at the expense of diamond miners and other workers, who may face harsh treatment and violations of their human rights.

However, in 2023 the General Assembly adopted a resolution on 'The role of diamonds in fuelling conflict: breaking the link between the illicit transaction of rough diamonds and armed conflict as a contribution to the prevention and resolution of conflicts',[22] which recognized that the KPCS contributes to the effective implementation of relevant Security Council resolutions containing sanctions on the trade in conflict diamonds, and called for the full implementation of existing Council measures to that end.

Tony Allen (1940–2020), a Nigerian Afrobeat drummer who played for a long time with Fela Kuti, sings about the precariousness of migrations to Europe in 'Boat Journey' (2014):

> Running away from misery
> And you can find yourself in a double misery
> You don't decide to leave your misery behind
> From the past it was shown in your country
> Now you jump into the boat
> To cross the ocean with all your family
> Looking, looking for better situation across the ocean
> But you never arrive
> Don't take the boat journey, my brothers!
> Don't take the boat journey, my sisters!

A world of its own is the work of Bob Dylan, which cannot be dealt with in this chapter; let me just say that his songs provide a rich and multifaceted exploration of many international law issues such as war, peace, human rights

22 Document A/78/L.54.

and the human condition, through both direct ('John Brown', 'Highway 61', 'Masters of War', 'With God on Our Side', 'Let Me Die in My Footsteps', 'Slow Train', 'Neighborhood Bully') and metaphorical ('It's Alright, Ma (I'm Only Bleeding)', 'A Hard Rain's A-Gonna Fall', 'Gates of Eden', 'Pay in Blood') arguments. Bob Dylan's work demonstrates a deep understanding of international law and the dynamics of international relations, including insights into the underlying causes of war, the links between profit motives and pro-war approaches, the inherent fragility of alliances between States, and the notion that wars often represent 'mistakes of past history' ('Footsteps'), and helps to describe the landscape in which international law exists.[23]

Also in Italy, the alternative rock band Consorzio Suonatori Indipendenti (CSI) mentions the UN and NATO in 'Cupe vampe' [Dark Flames] when talking about the destruction of Sarajevo and its library:

Cupe vampe, livide stanze
Occhio cecchino etnico assassino
Alto il sole, sete e sudore
Piena la luna, nessuna fortuna
Ci fotte la guerra che armi non ha
Ci fotte la pace che ammazza qua e là
Ci fottono i preti, i pope, i mullah
L'ONU, la NATO, la civiltà
Bella la vita dentro un catino
Bersaglio mobile di ogni cecchino
Bella la vita a Sarajevo città
Questa è la favola della viltà

Dark flames, livid rooms
Sniper eye, ethnic killer
The sun is high, thirst and sweat
Full moon, no luck
We are fucked by a war that doesn't have weapons
We are fucked by a peace that kills here and there
We are fucked by priests, popes, mullahs
By UN, NATO, civilization
Life is beautiful inside a basin
Moving target of every sniper
Life is beautiful in Sarajevo city
This is the tale of cowardice

As is known, the city of Sarajevo, today's capital of Bosnia and Herzegovina, suffered the longest siege of a capital in the history of modern warfare, a siege that lasted 1,425 days (from April 1992 to February 1996), during the Bosnian War, which was part of the Yugoslav wars that took place between 1991 and 2001, after the dissolution of the Socialist Federal Republic of Yugoslavia (SFRY). The International Criminal Tribunal for the former Yugoslavia declared it to be an international conflict, in particular between the Bosnian

23 For a wider analysis, see M. L. Perlin, 'You That Build the Death Planes': Bob Dylan, War and International Affairs', 28 April 2019, https://ssrn.com/abstract=3379255.

army and the army of the Serb Republic of Bosnia and Herzegovina, which aimed to annex the whole of Bosnia and Herzegovina. At the same time, it was established that the Croatian Republic of Herzeg-Bosnia was actively participating in the conflict with the same goal, namely the annexation of a part of the Bosnian territory.

The agreement that put an end to the conflict (signed in Paris on December 14, 1995) established the inviolability of the borders, which, in application of the *uti possidetis* rule, were the same as the borders between the federated republics of the SFRY, and provided for the creation of two entities within the State of Bosnia and Herzegovina: Croatian Federation (Muslim, covering 51% of the Bosnian territory, with 92 municipalities), and Republika Srpska (49% of the territory with 64 municipalities): the two entities created are endowed with autonomous powers in large sectors, but are integrated into a unified State framework.

The agreement also provided for the transfer or return to Croatia of Eastern Slavonia, which had been occupied by Serbian forces until the end of the war, and for the return of refugees to their Countries of origin.

International Law in the Heavy Metal Context: A Brief Introduction

The cultural representations of law, and of international law in particular, are, as I have tried to show, innumerable and diverse. They range from those written, thought and enjoyed by professionals, such as textbooks, commentaries and decisions, to those that tell about international law in the most diverse cultural fields, such as cinema, literature[24], comics and so on.

What I'll try to do now is to understand whether heavy metal as a musical genre offers a representation of international law that is somehow oriented, that is to say if it reconstructs that specific legal phenomenon (or, more precisely, some of its *factual* elements) with the aim of highlighting only *some* of its aspects, be they positive or negative.

This, I am aware, is certainly not a peculiarity of the representation of the phenomenon within music, since similar approaches are used in the most diverse contexts: one may think of the case of politics, with narratives aimed at promoting the change of a certain context of power or its maintenance, as in the case of sovereignisms.

24 The novels written by Philip Sands are completely peculiar since their author, in addition to being a writer, is also an internationalist legal scholar, and his novels deal with family stories deeply connected to historical events in which international law plays a central role.

I will therefore try to understand if and how a certain musical approach can influence the way in which aspects of issues regulated by international law, and thus indirectly *international law itself*, are narrated in the context of some extreme music.

Obviously, the social, cultural and economic context in which a given phenomenon is born, grows and develops significantly determines its basic characteristics: let's just remember that heavy metal was born in the Western world, particularly in the English-speaking world, and is characterised by the desire to react to established authority (listen to British Judas Priest, 'Breaking the Law', 1980), to express the discomfort of certain social classes, particularly those belonging to the white race and the working class, or to emphasise power itself, even for parodic or critical purposes (listen to Anthrax, from New York, 'I Am the Law', 1986, inspired by the comic character of Judge Dredd).

Curiously, however, when the genre goes global (and this has been happening since the late 1980s), and especially when it arrives in very different socially and culturally areas, such as Eastern Europe, Africa, Asia or South America, it takes on very specific characteristics, which, by emphasising its attitude of protest, assume a quite different social role from the one it had in the contexts of origin. These characteristics influence the way in which legally relevant facts, and especially those of international relevance, are told.

Furthermore, the success of a particular musical genre in a particular context is very significant.

The popularity of heavy metal – which, as I said, has always been a niche genre in the West – in developing Countries like India, Poland, Belarus, Estonia and Lithuania and all the former Soviet republics, but also in many Middle Eastern Countries (where it is often banned), indicates a desire for social change, westernisation or a response/reaction to globalisation (the latter, as we'll see, seems to be a very strong theme in some Brazilian heavy metal).

Again, I have to remind you that my discourse will be purely case-based and transversal to metal subgenres, since the limits of this chapter do not allow me to make a specific subdivision.

International Law in Heavy Metal: Some Western Cases

In a society that values order, there is a tendency to suppress disorder, while heavy metal music brings chaotic imagery to the forefront, invigorating these themes through its dynamic sound.

In contrast to the protest songs I spoke of in the former paragraph, which typically reject the violence associated with warfare, many heavy metal bands compose specific tracks that vividly depict distinct military actions. These songs often portray soldiers valiantly engaged in combat on the battlefield, exhibiting bravery and resilience while operating behind enemy lines, or participating in counterattacks, military sieges, lethal bombings and tank manoeuvres, probably also due to the musical characteristics of the genre.[25]

But while some heavy metal bands' representations of warfare are efforts to underscore the chaos and destruction inherent in conflict, without expressing scepticism regarding the underlying motivations for war,[26] some others express their criticism on those issues.

The world-famous British band Iron Maiden, always opens their concerts playing a recording of Churchill's speech of 4 June 1940

> We shall go on to the end, we shall fight in France, we shall fight on the seas and oceans, we shall fight with growing confidence and growing strength in the air, we shall defend our Island, whatever the cost may be, we shall fight on the beaches, we shall fight on the landing grounds, we shall fight in the fields and in the streets, we shall fight in the hills; we shall never surrender!

and plays several songs that reflect themes related to international law, particularly in the context of war, conflict and human rights, often explored through historical narratives and personal experiences of soldiers.

'Aces High' (1984) reflects the experiences of pilots during World War II, emphasising the psychological and physical toll of war. It focusses on aerial combat and the heroism of fighter pilots, encompassing legal and ethical implications of aerial bombardments and the protection of non-combatants.

> There goes the siren that warns of the air raid
> Then comes the sound of the guns sending flak
> Out for the scramble, we've got to get airborne
> Got to get up for the coming attack
> Jump in the cockpit and start up the engines

---

25 S. Puri, 'Machine Guns and Machine Gun Drums: Heavy Metal's Portrayal of War', in *Heavy Fundamentalisms: Music, Metal and Politics,* eds. R. Hill and K. Spracklen (Freeland: Inter-Disciplinary Press, 2010): 55.

26 'Since the dawn of time, men have waged war, and always there was the music. Horns and drums, lyres and pipes inspired and preceded men into battle; bards celebrated victory, lamented defeat'; R. Soodalter, 'Legends: Sing a Song of War', www.historynet.com/legends-sing-song-war.

Remove all the wheelblocks, there's no time to waste
Gathering speed as we head down the runway
Got to get airborne before it's too late

'The Trooper' (1983) draws inspiration from the Charge of the Light Brigade, a military action undertaken on 25 October 1854 by British light cavalry against Russian forces during the Battle of Balaclava in the Crimean War, resulting in many casualties to the cavalry, also chanted by Alfred Tennyson's narrative poem 'The Charge of the Light Brigade' (1854) published six weeks after the event.

The song raises questions about the conduct of armed forces and the principles of distinction and proportionality in warfare, which are central to the Geneva Conventions.

The bugle sounds, the charge begins
But on this battlefield, no one wins
The smell of acrid smoke and horses' breath
As I plunge on into certain death

In 'Run to the Hills' (1982), they address the impact of colonisation of North America and the displacement of indigenous peoples, with a critical approach to colonisation and the violations of human rights that accompanied it.

White man came across the sea
He brought us pain and misery
He killed our tribes, he killed our creed
He took our game for his own need
We fought him hard, we fought him well
Out on the plains we gave him hell
But many came, too much for Cree
Oh, will we ever be set free?

The themes of dispossession and violence resonate with international legal frameworks that seek to protect the rights of indigenous populations and address historical injustices, such as the United Nations Declaration on the Rights of Indigenous Peoples. The narrative in 'Run to the Hills' serves as a reminder of the legal obligations that States have towards indigenous communities, particularly in terms of self-determination and cultural preservation.

The music of the Swedish band Sabaton, known for dealing solely with historical themes and military narratives to the point that they even lead a

YouTube Channel explaining all the historical background to their music,[27] is even more linked to international law, particularly in the context of armed conflict and humanitarian principles. Also, Sabaton's songs often reflect on the experiences of soldiers and the moral complexities of war, which can serve as a lens through which to examine the implications of international humanitarian law (IHL). The narratives presented in Sabaton's music evoke IHL protections and some legal considerations surrounding warfare; the role of their music in shaping the perception of war and its legal ramifications for their fans is significant. Music can be a powerful medium that influences ethnonationalist sentiments and can even be weaponised in conflicts. This suggests that Sabaton's music, while primarily a form of entertainment, participates in a broader discourse about the legality of war. The band's constant focus on historical battles and military events reminds us of the legal frameworks that govern such conflicts, emphasising the necessity of compliance with international law to prevent atrocities and protect human rights.

The examples could be numerous. Their 'The Christmas Truce' (2021) is a poignant tribute to the series of unofficial ceasefires that occurred in the days around Christmas 1914 in various areas of the Western Front of World War I. As early as the week before Christmas, members of the German and British troops, stationed on opposite sides of the front, began exchanging greetings and carols from their respective trenches and occasionally crossed the lines to bring gifts to soldiers on the other side. On Christmas Eve and Christmas Day, large numbers of soldiers from German and British units (and, to a lesser extent, French) spontaneously left the trenches to meet in no-man's land to fraternise, exchange food and souvenirs. In addition to celebrating common religious and funeral ceremonies for the fallen, soldiers from both sides maintained friendly relations to the point of organising *impromptu* soccer matches.

> Silence
> Oh, I remember the silence
> On a cold winter day
> After many months on the battlefield
> And we were used to the violence
> Then all the cannons went silent
> And the snow fell
> Voices sang to me from no man's land
>
> And today we're all brothers
> Tonight we're all friends

27 www.youtube.com/SabatonHistory.

A moment of peace in a war that never ends
Today we're all brothers
We drink and unite
Now Christmas has arrived and the snow turns the ground white
Hear carols from the trenches, we sing O holy night
Our guns laid to rest among snowflakes
A Christmas in the trenches, a Christmas on the front far from home

The music of Slayer, thrash band from Los Angeles, particularly the song 'Angel of Death' (1986), serves as a provocative exploration of issues that resonate deeply with IHL. It addresses the atrocities committed during World War II, with a particular focus on the actions of Josef Mengele at Auschwitz, vividly illustrating the violation of these principles by recounting the inhumane medical experiments carried out on prisoners:

Auschwitz, the meaning of pain
The way that I want you to die
Slow death, immense decay
Showers that cleanse you of your life

Forced in like cattle, you run
Stripped of your life's worth
Human mice, for the Angel of Death
Four hundred thousand more to die

Pumped with fluid, inside your brain
Pressure in your skull begins pushing through your eyes
Burning flesh, drips away
Test of heat burns your skin, your mind starts to boil
Frigid cold, cracks your limbs

IHL is a set of international law rules which aim to limiting the effects of armed conflict. It protects mostly persons who are not or are no longer participating in the hostilities and restricts the means and methods of warfare.

A major part of IHL is contained in the four Geneva Conventions of 1949 that been developed and supplemented by two further agreements: the Additional Protocols of 1977 relating to the protection of victims of armed conflicts. Many provisions of IHL are now accepted as general international law.

Metallica, probably the world's most famous heavy metal band, in their 'One' (1988, which is inspired by the 1938 novel 'Johnny Got His Gun' by

Dalton Trumbo), tell the story of a young soldier who, injured by a landmine, loses his limbs and senses during World War I, ultimately becoming trapped in his own body while yearning for communication and connection. Not only the lyrics, but also the music mirrors the soldier's internal turmoil, transitioning from a sombre reflection on his condition to a powerful crescendo that conveys the intensity of his anguish, emphasising the brutality of war and showcasing not only the physical injuries sustained but also the psychological scars that accompany such trauma. This duality of experience – both the physical and mental toll of warfare – serves to critique the glorification of combat and the often-overlooked consequences faced by veterans.

> Fed through the tube that sticks in me
> Just like a wartime novelty
> Tied to machines that make me be
> Cut this life off from me
>
> Landmine has taken my sight
> Taken my speech
> Taken my hearing
> Taken my arms
> Taken my legs
> Taken my soul
> Left me with life in hell

International law prohibits the use of anti-personnel mines through the Convention on the Prohibition of the Use, Stockpiling, Production and Transfer of Anti-Personnel Mines and on their Destruction, signed in Ottawa in 1997. The Convention represents a significant step towards deterring the use of such weapons, establishing a global ban that has been ratified by 156 States to date. The Convention imposes international law obligations in order to limit the serious humanitarian and environmental consequences of anti-personnel mines, which continue to cause civilian victims even years after the end of conflicts. Anti-personnel mines produce an indiscriminate impact, affecting not only soldiers but also civilians, in particular women and children, and hindering the reconstruction of societies affected by war. However, not all Countries have joined the treaty: for example, the United States, despite having adopted policies to limit the use of anti-personnel mines, has not ratified the Convention, maintaining an ambivalent position regarding the use of mines in specific contexts.

Also, Megadeth's 'Holy Wars… The Punishment Due' (1990) serves as a profound commentary on the complexities of war, particularly in the context of religious conflicts. The title itself encapsulates the dual themes of holy wars and the consequences that arise from such conflicts. The song reflects the historical and psychological dimensions of warfare, particularly how religion can be manipulated to justify violence and aggression. As known, the concept of holy war has been historically rooted in the idea of divine sanction for conflict, often framed as a form of punishment or protection. Some scholars discuss how holy wars are perceived as both punitive and protective measures, suggesting that such conflicts are often justified through a moral lens that aligns with religious beliefs:[28] this associates with the themes in Megadeth's lyrics, which critique the use of religion as a justification for violence. The song's narrative can be interpreted as a critique of how religious ideologies can lead to devastating consequences, echoing the sentiments on the humanitarian implications of war, where the justification of military interventions often leads to abuses.

> Brother will kill brother, spilling blood across the land
> Killing for religion, something I don't understand
> Fools like me who cross the sea and come to foreign lands
> Ask the sheep for their beliefs, 'Do you kill on God's command?'
> A country that's divided, surely will not stand
> My past erased, no more disgrace, no foolish naïve stand
> The end is near, it's crystal clear, part of the master plan
> Don't look now to Israel, it might be your homeland
> Holy wars

The song also raises the question of the relationship between religious freedom and international security. The United Nations Security Council, at least in the context of international terrorism, seems to be increasingly reading religion, or at least some radical visions of it – even if not openly, and indeed often with a series of clauses relating to the non-attribution of terrorism to any religion or culture, which, it must be said, often sound like *excusationes non petitae* – as an element, if I may use the expression, of a risk to security.

Now, while the free expression of one's beliefs falls with no doubt within the context of religious freedom, religious fanaticism, especially in its most radical forms, may not be compatible even with a broad interpretation of fundamental rights as protected by international law. In short, I think I can say that if, on the one hand, the latest practice of the Security Council in no way

28 J. Krašovec, 'The Holy War as Punishment and Protection', 310–338.

legitimises the link between terrorism and religions, on the other hand, this is most likely not true with regard to some extreme forms of religious expression that imply the total suppression of the rights of others, especially the right to life. It should be made clear that what I am saying does not apply *sic et simpliciter* to any religion that limits fundamental rights as they are conceived in the Western context (think, for example, of the relationship of some religions with women's freedoms), but only when the forms of expression, organisation, and imposition of a given religious sentiment have a negative impact on the hard core of fundamental rights, and in particular on the right to life. In such cases, it is likely that we are dealing with an abusive form of the exercise of religious freedom, which, as is well known, occurs when a right is exercised by its holder in a manner that is manifestly incompatible or contrary to the purpose for which it was conceived and recognized.

The relationships between heavy metal bands and legal doctrine may even be explicit: Exodus, an American thrash band, opens their 'Fabulous Disaster' full-length of 1989 with an excerpt from *Kind and Usual Punishment: The Prison Business* of Jessica Mitford,[29] which focuses on the conditions of prisoners and the inhumanity of prison.

> The prison system, inherently unjust and inhumane
> Is the ultimate expression of injustice
> And inhumanity in the society at large.
> Those of us on the outside do not like
> To think of wardens and guards as our surrogates, yet they are.
> And they are intimately locked in a deadly embrace
> With their human captives behind prison walls.
> By extension, so are we.
> The terrible double meaning is thus imparted
> To the original question of human ethics
> 'Am I my brother's keeper?'

Black metal, a genre that emerged in Norway in the early 1990s and is infamous for the bloody events that occurred within its inner circle,[30] is characterised by fast tempos, a shrieking vocal style, heavily distorted guitars played with tremolo picking, lo-fi recording, unconventional song structures, transgressive themes, anti-establishment sentiments and a complex

29 1973 (New York: Knopf, Distributed by Random House).

30 See M. Moynhian and D. Soderlind, *Lords of Chaos – The Bloody Rise of the Satanic Metal Underground* (Port Townsend: Feral House, 1998).

relationship with nature and the environment. The aesthetic and ideological underpinnings of this genre can be juxtaposed with international environmental law, particularly in the context of environmental policy and the broader impact of cultural expressions on environmental consciousness. Let me remind that one of the most influential records was named 'A Blaze in the Northern Sky' (Darkthrone, 1991), and another Norwegian band was named Carpathian Forest. Idealised landscapes are depicted on black metal album covers, with grainy flash photographs taken at night showing trees and snow, as in Darkthrone's 'Under a Funeral Moon' (1993), or naturalistic landscape photos, such as Enslaved's album 'Frost' (1994), showing a fog-shrouded fjord.

The genre's ultra-conservative approach to nature, depicted in its lyrics and imagery, reflects a deep connection to the environment, which is also a focus of environmental legislation. The Norwegian government has implemented many environmental laws that are in line with international standards, such as the precautionary and ecosystem approaches in fisheries legislation, which aim to balance ecological sustainability with economic interests.

Moreover, the black metal scene's engagement with themes of destruction and rebirth can be seen as a metaphor for environmental degradation and the need for restoration. The violent aesthetic often associated with the genre, including references to nature's fury, can serve as a critique of industrialisation and its impact on the environment. The black metal genre may thus serve as a platform for raising awareness of ecological issues, and its thematic focus on nature and rebellion provides a unique lens through which to examine the relationship between cultural expressions and international environmental law.

This reflects a broader trend in international environmental law, where cultural narratives, including those from music, can influence public perceptions and policymaking on environmental issues.

In the case of Orphaned Land, a band from Israel, the theme of Israeli-Palestinian coexistence is addressed, not only through the lyrics but perhaps above all through the music: the band is made up of Israeli musicians and offers a death metal with strong oriental and folk music influences, both Arab and Israeli (Mizrahi and Maghrebi Jewish, Arabic, Turkish and other Middle Eastern and North African musical elements, with particular influences from Yemenite Jewish and, in their early years, Moroccan Jewish music, as well as from Sephardic music and other sounds from the Mediterranean). They have also included metallized versions of various piyyutim in all of their albums. In the video clip for 'Like Orpehus'[31] they tell of Israeli-Palestinian coexistence

31 www.youtube.com/watch?v=hurWzo01FpM&ab_channel=CenturyMediaRecords.

through the common passion of young people from both groups for heavy metal:

> And this life is the pain of being born
> Man, child and woman all are one
> I sing before you all

Heavy Metal in the Global South: Some Examples

As I said, heavy metal music has evolved into a global phenomenon, with distinct scenes emerging in various regions, including the Global South, where the approach reflects local cultural, social and political contexts that differ significantly from the genre's origins in the Western States.

As we'll see by few examples, in the Global South, heavy metal often has served as a form of resistance against oppressive political regimes and social injustices: in Countries like Turkey it has been a vehicle for expressing dissent against authoritarianism and has become intertwined with the search for identity amidst the challenges of democratization, allowing for the articulation of diverse viewpoints that challenge the prevailing religious and nationalist narratives.

Moreover, the heavy metal scene in the Global South frequently grapples with issues of race and identity. Discourses of whiteness and masculinity are negotiated within heavy metal scenes in Countries like South Africa, where local musicians adapt the genre to reflect their unique cultural experiences, leading to a translocal narrative that illustrates how heavy metal can both reproduce and challenge existing power structures, allowing for a complex interplay between global influences and local realities.

Furthermore, musical expression is obviously conditioned by the exercise of fundamental rights: in this sense the story of Acrassiscauda, the first Iraqi metal band, is paradigmatic. Formed in Baghdad in 2001, they emerged as a significant cultural phenomenon amidst the backdrop of war and social upheaval in Iraq; they were featured in the documentary *Heavy Metal in Baghdad*, which chronicled their struggles and aspirations and highlighted the unique position of Iraqi metal musicians within the broader heavy metal community. The band's experiences reflect a broader narrative about the role of music in conflict zones. Just let me remind you that Taliban forbade instruments including the piano, the flute and the lute during their first period in power in Afghanistan (1996–2001), and ISIS likewise sought to eradicate un-Islamic instruments like the saxophone, drums and keyboard in Syria and Libya.

Also, the Brazilian heavy metal band Sepultura has often addressed themes that resonate with international law issues, particularly in the context of decolonisation, indigenous people's rights, human rights and environmental concerns. Their lyrics and music reflect a deep engagement with international law issues.

For instance, their album 'Roots' explores the struggles of indigenous peoples and the impact of colonialism.

'Kaiowas' is an instrumental song 'inspired by a Brazilian Indian tribe who lived in the rain forest' and, staying to the album liner notes, 'committed mass suicide as a protest against the Brazilian government', 'who took away their land and beliefs'. The truth is that the tribe wrote a letter to the Brazilian Government in order to protest, after an eviction order had been issued by a federal judge, in which they declared to be ready to accept their own extinction: 'We are already going to and want to be killed and buried along with our ancestors here where we are today, therefore, we ask the Government and the Federal Justice not to decree our eviction, but instead we request them to decree our mass death and to bury us all here. We ask them, once and for all, to decree our total decimation and extinction, besides sending many tractors to dig a large hole to drop and bury our bodies. This is our request to the federal judges. We already await this decision of the Federal Justice. Decree our mass death Guarani and Kaiowá of Pyelito Kus/Mbarakay and bury us here. Given that we fully decided it and won't leave this place dead or alive'.

Moreover, Sepultura's engagement with environmental issues is evident in their music, particularly in songs like 'Territory' (1993), which critiques the exploitation of natural resources and the consequences of such actions on local communities.

Unknown man
Speaks to the world
Sucking in your trust
A trap in every word
War for territory
War for territory

International law addresses land grabbing through various frameworks and mechanisms aimed at regulating land acquisition, protecting human rights and promoting sustainable development. The phenomenon of land grabbing, often characterized by large-scale land acquisitions by foreign entities or local elites, has raised significant concerns regarding human rights violations and environmental sustainability.

International law recognises land as a critical resource that must be managed responsibly. The UN established mechanisms to monitor and address human rights violations associated with large-scale land acquisitions: UN treaty bodies have documented numerous cases of human rights violations associated with land grabbing, highlighting the need for stronger governance frameworks to protect vulnerable populations.

The role of international organizations, such as the World Bank and the Food and Agriculture Organization (FAO), has also been crucial in shaping the discourse on land grabbing: these organizations have engaged in extensive research and stakeholder discussions to develop guidelines aimed at mitigating the negative impacts of land.

But domestic legal frameworks governing land transactions vary widely across Countries, resulting in a patchwork of regulations that can either facilitate or hinder land grabbing. In many developing Countries, weak legal protections for land rights, coupled with corruption and lack of enforcement, create an environment conducive to exploitative land transactions. The environmental impacts of land grabbing are also a critical concern in international law: research shows that land grabbing often leads to unsustainable agricultural practices, resulting in environmental degradation and biodiversity loss.

The theme of the relationship between population and territory is also addressed by another Brazilian thrash metal band, Tamuya Thrash Tribe,[32] which even titles one of its songs with a principle of international law such as 'Uti Possidetis' (2016).

Leave these lands
They still refuse
They want to die
With stupid pride
This war for territory
Will have to end
The kings agreed
To exchange our lands
We've been living here
For so many years
While they drink their wines
In golden glasses

---

32 I owe this reference to my colleague Anne Lagerwall, who spoke to me of this band during a seminar on Pop International Law we held together in Rome in November 2024.

But this is where we want to be
This is the land of the Guaranys
They should know this land was given to us
And freely we shall give to our heirs
Leave these lands
We still refuse
If we have to die
We'll die with pride

The legal principle of *uti possidetis* arises in the context of decolonization and the definition of State borders, originally in Latin America, and establishes that newly independent States inherit the existing territorial borders of the colonial entities from which they separated. The principle, which aims to avoid territorial conflicts and ensure stability in relations between new States, has also come under strong criticism for perpetuating artificial borders that do not reflect social and cultural realities.

Also, environmental issues can be found in Sepulura's 'Biotech is Godzilla' (1993):

Rio Summit, '92
Street people kidnapped, hid from view
'To save the Earth', our rulers met
Some had other secret plans

As known, the Rio Summit, the United Nations Conference on Environment and Development (UNCED) was an international summit which was held in Rio de Janeiro (Brazil) in June 1992 and represented one of the fundamental steps in the process of international environmental cooperation. It involved 172 governments, 108 heads of State and numerous non-governmental organizations, and produced the Rio Declaration, with which some key principles were established for achieving sustainable development in the world. According to the Declaration, the only way to achieve long-term economic growth is to ensure that it is inextricably linked to environmental protection. In particular, Principle 7 underlines how States have 'common but differentiated' responsibilities in the process of cooperation towards the protection and restoration of ecosystems, and Principle 15 requires the use of a precautionary approach in protecting the environment.

Africa, as for everything else, is too big and fragmented to be dealt with holistically, also when it comes to heavy metal, so I'll just limit to a few examples: it's worth noting that Brazilian Sepultura is one of the notable influences in the African heavy metal scene, under which the local scene evolved.

Before that, Witch, a '70s psych-rock band hailing from Zambia, are often credited as one of the pioneers of African rock and metal and blend traditional Zambian sounds with rock, creating a unique fusion which influenced the whole movement.[33]

The Nigerian metal scene has seen the rise of bands like Blood Covenant and The Toads, which incorporate local languages and themes into their music, tackling issues such as corruption, social inequality and the impact of colonialism.

Arka'n Asrafokor is a prominent heavy metal band from Togo that has gained recognition for its unique blend of traditional Togolese music and heavy metal influences. The band's name translates to [The sound of the people], reflecting their commitment to addressing social issues and cultural identity through their music. Their lyrical content often revolves around themes such as social justice, political struggles and the importance of cultural heritage, resonating deeply with the Togolese populace and beyond. Through their performances, they aim to inspire change and encourage dialogue about pressing social issues, making them not just musicians but also advocates for social justice.

Very briefly, in Asia we can find The Hu, a Mongolian folk metal band formed in 2016 in Ulan Bator, which has recently achieved global fame. The band fuses metal sounds with traditional Mongolian ones, using both the instruments and the language in its songs (listen to their 2019 song 'Yuve Yuve Yuve Yu', [The Song of the Eternal]), the band forcefully expresses the pride of its origins and the need not to passively suffer Western influence.

A (Little) Conclusion

Heavy metal music demonstrates a much more assiduous familiarity with issues of international law than is the case with 'generalist' pop music, probably due to the musical characteristics of the genre and its cosmopolitan approach.[34]

Furthermore, I think we can highlight a difference in approach between metal artists of Western origin and others.

The former, in a very general sense, seems to take approaches that are aligned with traditional interpretations of international law, seen as a

33 'Witch: We Intend To Cause Havoc' is a 2021 documentary that follows the formation of the band and documents the life of its lead singer, Jagari, whose name is an Africanisation of Mick Jagger's.

34 I refer to cosmopolitanism as the cultural formation of ideas, practices and technologies that bind together people from different locations and cultures.

substantially crystallised set of rules that should be respected and applied, rather than modified.

The bands coming from the Countries of the Global South propose a narrative of reaction to the existing power structures in international law, which are seen as aimed at perpetuating historical and contemporary inequalities between the Global North and South.

For them, international law is not a neutral system of rules between sovereign States, but has been historically shaped by colonial dynamics that continue today.

This interpretation bears a resemblance to the perspectives put forth by the contemporary doctrine known as Third World Approaches to International Law (TWAIL).

This critical school of thought, while not entirely homogeneous, constitutes both an intellectual and political movement that reads international law as a mechanism that perpetuates the exploitation of the Third World by maintaining its subordination to Western powers.

Scholars affiliated with TWAIL, often referred to as TWAILers, aim to address and reform what they perceive as the oppressive dimensions of international law by revisiting its colonial underpinnings. Furthermore, it has been noted that the TWAIL movement itself has been significantly influenced by scholars from Europe and North America, despite its claims to represent the interests of the Third World. It has been observed that a substantial portion of TWAIL scholarship originates from and is disseminated within the Global North. Additionally, the majority of TWAIL conferences and events have been organised and financed by institutions based in the Global North, even in instances where these gatherings have occurred in the Global South.

Even in this, I think we can spot a similarity with the heavy metal currents from the Global South, which too, as we have seen, were born in the English-speaking Global North and then spread to the South and incorporated its demands.

All the songs I cited can be listened to just by scanning this QR code, that will lead you to the 'Doing international law with earbuds' playlist.

Chapter 7

THE MULTIPLE CHARACTERS OF FRANCISCO IBÁÑEZ TALAVERA AND THE LAW

Antoni Abat i Ninet*

The Cultural Transcendence of Francisco Ibáñez and His Multiple Characters

Writing about the multiple characters of Francisco Ibáñez necessarily involves reflecting on a cultural phenomenon that far transcended the design of characters and comics. Consequently, law, in its holistic nature, was not immune to the effects of this phenomenon, which humorously and sarcastically depicted society at a specific moment in time. In fact, the law and the political system, with its lights and shadows, are the predominant subjects of the satirical critique that Ibáñez addresses in his comics. This is true both during the late stages of the Franco dictatorship (in its progressively more open phase), the democratic transition (a totem and taboo in the Freudian sense in Spain)[1] and in more recent times. It is not only that his comics gained widespread popularity in Spain, amassing thousands of readers, but also that 'we, the readers', experienced a cultural transformation – perhaps even existential – when confronted with an Ibáñez comic. It is no exaggeration to describe Francisco Ibáñez as one of the most important cultural figures of the last 50 years.[2]

* All websites accessed on 15 October 2024

1 S. Freud, A. Arden Brill, and Sigmund Freud Collection, *Totem and Taboo; Resemblances Between the Psychic Lives of Savages and Neurotics* (New York: Moffat, Yard and Company, 1918).

2 J. Rubio Hancock, '11 escenas que pasan en todas las historietas de Mortadelo y Filemón', Verne, 8 October 2015, https://verne.elpais.com/verne/2015/10/07/articulo/1444202259_203587.html.

Culture can be defined as a symbolic process through which human beings cognitively order reality and transmit their ways of life. Human beings are creatures of culture, having culture-specific orientations to reality (i.e. forms of consciousness) and culture-induced motivations that vary across history, types of societies and individual experience.[3] Ibáñez clearly contributed to this symbolic process of ordering reality and conveying a specific way of life. To understand the phenomenon of Ibáñez and other cartoonists in Spain, and to fully appreciate the tremendous merit they had, some historical context is required. As a matter of example, in terms of means of communication, in the 1970s, not everyone had a TV, or the signal didn't reach their home, and it was during this time that the two public broadcast channels began transitioning to colour. Ibáñez was able to bring smiles to the faces of both children and adults, regardless of age or location, making us happy as we imaginatively interacted with and sympathised with his characters. Not to mention, many children developed the habit of reading through his comics, and as Ibáñez himself expressed: 'some of them may have ended up reading Kafka and Kant'.[4] Well, I am one of these kids, as are many of my colleagues in the universities of Spain.

Ibáñez's impact was even greater for Generation X (those born between 1965 and 1980), a generation that witnessed Spain's democratic transformation and transition. This period marked the end of Francoist censorship (from 1975) and the emergence of freedom of expression and press. As the artist himself mentioned in multiple interviews, censorship affected how writers and artists expressed their work, and Ibáñez, despite drawing characters, was no exception. He explained that the use of very silly expressions by his characters was due to censorship: 'That group of thugs would come to the editorial offices, and the friendliest among them looked like he had killed his father and mother – what could you do? At least, they gave us a tremendous variety of vocabulary'.[5]

3 L. Greenfeld and E. Malczewski, 'Politics as a Cultural Phenomenon', in *Handbook of Politics: State and Society in Global Perspective*, eds. K. T. Leicht and J. Craig Jenkins (New York: Springer, 2010).

4 V. Drake, '¿Por qué Francisco Ibáñez borró a los políticos de sus viñetas?', ABC, 18 July 2023, https://www.abc.es/xlsemanal/a-fondo/entrevista-francisco-ibanez-politicos-mortadelo-filemon-rompetechos.html?x-vocento-user-type=anonimo&x-vocento-hide-content=no&x-vocento-access-type=ALLOW_ACCESS/.

5 J. Blánquez, 'Ibáñez: "La censura no me dejaba usar palabras como culo en Mortadelo y Filemón"', El Mundo, 17 November 2017, https://www.elmundo.es/papel/cultura/2017/11/17/5a0db5bfe2704ea07e8b45ad.html.

The way to evade censorship was not only evident in the vocabulary (in form) but also in the content. Many of the messages in the comics were subliminal, implicit, suggestive or required a specific interpretation from the reader. Ibáñez also acknowledged a significant difference between his characters from the dictatorship era and those from afterwards. He stated: 'At first, the stories were very childish, but as the years went by, adults, not children, came to the signings. A huge, terrifying difference! So, I had to create something a bit more complex'.[6] A thematic evolution, increasingly politicised and less subtle, which the writer Francisco Umbral openly criticised when he stated that: 'Ibañez has decided to politicise his comics because slapstick humour no longer makes anyone laugh'.[7] The criticism is somewhat flawed because it seems to overlook the fact that Ibáñez, while maintaining his characteristic slapstick humour, did introduce elements of social and political critique, especially in his works during Spain's democratic transition and in the following decades. Although his comics are not intended to be profound political treatises, it is undeniable that they reflect and satirise the political and social realities of his time. This critical dimension may go unnoticed due to his humorous approach, but it is part of the richness of his comics. Therefore, to claim that his work lacks political depth oversimplifies its cultural impact. On the other hand, a minimally interested reading of Ibáñez's work, even from his so-called by Umbral 'political phase', reveals that our author has never abandoned the slapstick humour that, contrary to Umbral's opinion, still makes millions of readers around the world laugh.[8]

Antoni Guiral is right when he contends that comic series have always contained a dose of social and political criticism, a more veiled criticism until the seventies due to Franco's harsh censorship, which regulated comics very strictly. In Spain, more or less at the twilight of Franco's dictatorship, a renewal movement in comics emerged – first timidly and then more forcefully – both in formal aspects and, above all, in subject matter. This renewal came almost ten years later than in other Countries such as the United States or France and overlapped with the political transition from Francisco Franco's dictatorial regime to the current democracy.[9]

The combination of the renewal of comics and the emergence of freedoms led to a real boom in the medium that resulted in the social penetration of

6 Ibid.

7 Chespiro, 'Francisco Umbral habla sobre Francisco Ibañez', Mortadelo y Algo Más, 27 September 2009, https://mortadeloyalgomas.blogspot.com/2009/09/franciso-umbral-habla-sobre-francisco.html.

8 Ibid.

9 F. Lladó, *Los cómics de la transición. El Boom del cómic adulto 1975–1984* (Barcelona: Glénat, 2001).

comics and a certain levelling with literature and other artistic media.[10] This can be seen in the proliferation of publications, salons and exhibitions all over Spain. However, this process did not take more than ten years to abate, as demonstrated by the closure of almost all the comic magazines.[11] With the arrival of democracy, Ibáñez, along with his colleagues and characters, was liberated, allowing him to explore these themes with greater freedom, which led to the creation of some of his best albums. While there is always a parodic tone reflecting reality, there is also a surrealist tone, especially in the first adventures.[12]

As mentioned before, throughout his work, Ibáñez reflected our society, mirroring our streets. Despite Francisco Ibáñez's repeated assertion that his work (*Mortadelo and Filemón*) has no message, that nothing is hidden behind their adventures, and that the only intention of his comics is to make people laugh and forget about everything else, the reality is that, whether the author intended it or not, the adventures of Mortadelo and Filemón provide one of the most schizophrenic and irreverent portraits ever created of post-transition Spain. While obviously exaggerated, these adventures contain a significant dose of truth.[13] Behind the caricature taken to the limit – of slave-like working conditions, clumsy and corrupt politicians, street hustling and general shoddiness – lies a mirror in which Spain reflects its miseries, and which we all recognise: labour reforms, corruption scandals, mafias and criminals settled in Spain and a significantly improved functioning of the administrations.[14]

In this sense, the overwhelming success of the comics led to the need to officially deny that the secret agents (some of the most inept that could have ever existed) were members of the Spanish intelligence agency, CNI (*Centro Nacional de Inteligencia*). Some feared that the popularity of the comics might affect the public's perception of real Spanish secret agents.[15] This assertion doesn't seem far-fetched, given that, in fact, their caricaturing has been

10 M. López Rodriguez, *La narración gráfica, Ibáñez y Mortadelo y Filemón* (Granada: Universidad de Granada, 2016): 140.

11 Ibid.

12 G. Domínguez, 'Mortadelo y Filemón han sido un espejo de los temas de la calle', Público, 31 August 2011, https://www.publico.es/actualidad/mortadelo-y-filemon-han-sido.html.

13 N. Carretero, 'Mortadelo y Filemón, espejo de España', Yorokobu, 28 April 2014, https://www.yorokobu.es/mortadelo-y-filemon/.

14 Ibid.

15 J. Orcajada del Castillo, 'Mortadelo y Filemón no pertenecen al CNI', noticias de Navarra, 13 June 2016, https://www.noticiasdenavarra.com/opinion/2022/06/13/mortadelo-filemon-pertenecen-cni-4662447.html.

used with political slogans to discredit the agency, the real one.[16] However, viewed from another perspective, they might have become the most beloved law enforcement officials in history. This was exemplified by the Ministry of Finance, which chose the characters Mortadelo and Filemón for a campaign that reminded taxpayers of their obligation to request a receipt for all purchases or repairs, between October and November of 1995.[17] This caricaturing was not limited to the national reality. On the contrary, Mortadelo and Filemón added a touch of humour to the most significant events on the world stage, such as in the Maastricht… Jesus! album, which allowed us to look at the construction of the European Union with a smile, the arrival of the Euro or climate change.[18] To this, it can be also mentioned the parody of Pinochet or the bump on the head that the secret agents caused to Donald Trump when clumsily mishandling a drone.[19]

Ibáñez was very prolific throughout his long career, which started publicly in 1952, with the comic strip *Mucho ruido y pocas nueces*, and lasted practically the date of his death, 15 July 2023. It is widely acknowledged that Francisco Ibáñez's rise began with the publication of his characters Mortadelo and Filemón, published for the first time in 1958, and also with the publication of other important titles, whether due to their success or their representation of the sociopolitical context of the time. Such was the case with *Los Pérez*, *La familia Trapisonda* and *Rompetechos*, which started as a satirical reflection of the average Spaniard but ended up becoming a reflection of what was happening in many Countries around the world. Special mention goes to *13, Rue del Percebe*, first published in 1961, which some consider to be his crowning work.[20]

The transcendence of Ibáñez's characters is evidenced by the fact that his comics have been translated into multiple languages, including Catalan, French, Italian, Portuguese, German, Tagalog, Indonesian, Czech, Polish, Russian, Serbo-Croatian and Slovenian, among others, with the names of

16 Elindependiente, 'Aragonès compara al CNI con Mortadelo y Filemón por ponerlo al frente de los CDR', DailyMotion, January 2024, https://www.dailymotion.com/video/x8rta0n.

17 M. L. López Rodriguez, *La narración gráfica, Ibáñez y Mortadelo y Filemón* (Granada: Universidad de Granada, 2016): 414.

18 P. Diago Diago, 'Tebeos y Dipr: Homenaje a Francisco Ibáñez', Millennium DiPr, https://www.millenniumdipr.com/n-631-tebeos-y-dipr-homenaje-a-francisco-ibanez.

19 P. Quinteros, 'Murió Francisco Ibáñez Talavera, legendario creador de Mortadelo y Filemón que parodió a Pinochet', La Tercera, 16 July 2023, https://www.latercera.com/mouse/murio-francisco-ibanez-talavera-legendario-creador-de-mortadelo-y-filemon-que-parodio-a-pinochet/.

20 Ibid.

the protagonists changed in each Country. He has sold more than one hundred million copies. His comic on the Paris Olympic Games of 2024 (the last one he wrote) made him a 44-year Olympic cartoonist, as Mortadelo and Filemón have 'attended' every Games since Moscow 1980.[21]

Ibáñez's humour has also been reflected in cinematography – the first film premiered in 2003 with Javier Fresser as the director, *Mortadelo y Filemón, la gran aventura* (which by 2021 had more than five million viewers in Spain), the second in 2008, *Misión: Salvar la Tierra* with Miguel Bardem and the third and only animated one in 2014, *Mortadelo y Filemón contra Jimmy el Cachondo*, also directed by Fresser. In all the films, Ibáñez had some level of involvement and participation.[22] The characters have been the focus of multiple marketing campaigns, including books, computer games, major advertising campaigns ranging from financial institutions to the public telephone company, charity races and merchandising in the form of figurines, puzzles and even food products.[23]

In 2000, Mortadelo and Filemón were appointed official ambassadors for childhood by UNICEF. The following year, 2001, Francisco Ibáñez was awarded the *Medalla de Oro al Mérito en las Bellas Artes*, a medal that distinguishes individuals and entities that have excelled in the field of artistic and cultural creation and have rendered notable services in the promotion, development, or dissemination of art and culture, or in the preservation of artistic heritage.[24] In 2022, Ibáñez received the *Creu de Sant Jordi* from the Catalan Government, which recognises individuals or entities for their outstanding contributions to Catalonia in defence of its identity or in the civic and cultural sphere.[25]

After he passed away in 2023, the acts of recognition continued and even intensified, as he received the Gold Medal of the City of Barcelona for Cultural Merit. A newly opened public library, the García Márquez Library in Sant Martí (awarded in 2023 as the best new public library in the world),[26]

---

21 'La Página No Oficial de Mortadelo y Filemón', https://mortadelo-filemon.es/.

22 P. Diago Diago, 'Tebeos y Dipr: Homenaje a Francisco Ibáñez'.

23 M. L. López Rodriguez, *La narración gráfica, Ibáñez y Mortadelo y Filemón* (Granada: Universidad de Granada, 2016): 422.

24 'Medallas de Oro al Mérito en las Bellas Artes', Real Academia de Bellas Artes de San Fernando, 27 December 2012, https://www.realacademiabellasartessanfernando.com/noticias/academia/medallas-de-oro-al-merito-en-las-bellas-artes/

25 'Creus de Sant Jordi', Departament de la Presidència, https://presidencia.gencat.cat/ca/ambits_d_actuacio/premis/creus-de-sant-jordi/index.html.

26 P. Morehart, 'Barcelona Library Named Best New Public Library in the World', ilovelibraries, 29 August 2023, https://ilovelibraries.org/article/barcelona-library-named-best-new-public-library-in-the-world/.

which he had personally inaugurated, dedicated a permanent space to his vast body of work, and the neighbourhood where Ibáñez lived were *Mortadelo and Filemón* in the traffic lights.[27] Ibáñez passed away at the age of 87, worked every day and, without making a big deal out of it, would insist: 'I'm not a great artist, I wish I were'.[28]

It is not feasible to explore every character that Ibáñez created and analyse their legal significance in depth due to the sheer volume and complexity of his work – not even the multiple legal implications and references present in the more than 220 comics of Mortadelo and Filemón. The proposed analysis will specifically focus on particular comics that include explicit legal references or content, examining how the antics and interactions of its characters reflect and satirise various aspects of politics and law. The legal implications of these secret agents are divided into a domestic dimension (where Ibáñez addresses topics such as corruption, the law of the jury, government and many others) and an international (private and public) law dimension, despite our agreement with Diago when she mentions that in the world of humour, everything is international.

The space limitation of this chapter does not allow us to delve into select characters from *13, Rue del Percebe*, where some face legal troubles. One notable example is *Manolo el moroso* (the delinquent tenant) in the attic, whose life is a constant escape from his creditors. He employs very unique methods, such as spaceships, termites, floods and counterfeit bills, to humorously reflect the lack of effectiveness of court executions in collecting unpaid debts.[29]

On the third floor are the thief Ceferino Raffles and his wife. He is a small-time crook who can steal anything from handbags and trunks to the Christmas Lottery drum or from the shopkeeper Don Semen, whose grocery store is adjacent to the entrance. Ceferino is a master at inventing schemes to deceive customers regarding the weight and quality of his products, such as placing a magnet under the scale.[30] These are just a few examples of a

27 A. Abella, 'Homenaje y un beso en todo el 'colodrillo' para Francisco Ibáñez', El Periódico, 04 October 2024, https://www.elperiodico.com/es/ocio-y-cultura/20231004/homenaje-francisco-ibanez-medalla-oro-barcelona-garcia-marquez-92908347.

28 V. Drake, '¿Por qué Francisco Ibáñez borró a los políticos de sus viñetas?'.

29 P. Brachfield, 'La imposible ejecución judicial de Manolo el moroso de "13 Rue del Percebe"', Brachfield Credit & Risk Consultants, 12 November, 2019, https://perebrachfield.com/blog/noticias-e-informaciones/la-imposible-ejecucion-judicial-de-manolo-el-moroso-de-13-rue-del-percebe/.

30 A. Abella, '¿Quién es quién en "13, Rue del Percebe"?', El Periódico, 1 March 2016, https://www.elperiodico.com/es/ocio-y-cultura/20160301/13-rue-percebe-integral-tebeo-ibanez-4935005.

fantastic comic that, with a humorous and exaggerated tone, captures the different realities experienced in the buildings of any major city in Spain.

Mortadelo and Filemón, Secret Agents

These are the two secret agents that worked for the fictional organisation the T.I.A. (playing on the reference to the CIA and the Spanish meaning of 'TIA' which means 'aunt'). Its mission is to serve and protect citizens from criminals, although due to its incompetence, it is almost as harmful as the crooks themselves. Mortadelo wore a tall top hat and always carried an umbrella; Filemón dressed in a tweed jacket, a short-brimmed hat and smoked a pipe. A satire of Sherlock Holmes and Dr Watson, not only in appearance but also in their clumsy yet lucky case-solving.[31]

Mortadelo and Filemón follow the emerging trend of series featuring two protagonists, marking one of the great achievements in post-war graphic storytelling as they faithfully reflect the professional tensions of the time. From the friendly duality typical of late 1940s series – such as Carpanta-Protasio, Doña Urraca-Caramillo, Leovigilda-Hermenegilda, etc. – the early 1950s saw a shift toward a labour-related duality reflecting conflicts with domestic service, as in *Petra, criada* (servant) *para todo* by Escobar (1954), *Pascual, criado leal* by Nadal (1953) and *El Dr Cataplasma* by Martz Schmidt (1953). All of these would soon be surpassed by series that dealt with the opposition between boss and subordinate, employer and worker and so forth. This trend was initiated in 1951 by *Apolino Tarúguez* and culminated in series like *Mortadelo and Filemón* (1958) and others. In this style, Francisco Ibáñez would eventually become a true master.[32]

The basic personality traits of the two detectives were essentially the same from the beginning: Filemón, the 'boss' of the agency, always serious and bad-tempered, inevitably ends up taking the brunt of the mishaps caused by his partner; Mortadelo, well-meaning but somewhat inept, is always as skilled and quick with disguises as the famed Count of Monte Cristo. The duo can also be seen as a pair of clowns, with Filemón taking on the role of the serious and authoritarian clown, and Mortadelo as the 'auguste', the one who dresses

31 L. M. Cruz, 'Francisco Ibáñez: Leyenda de la historieta española', 17 July 2023, https://radixanimacion.com/figuras/trayectoria-francisco-ibanez/.

32 'Capitulo 1 – El Nacimiento de un Mito', La Página no Oficial de Mortadelo y Filemón, https://mortadelo-filemon.es/content?q=Y2F0X2lkPTQ4JmN0Z19pZD0xMDkmcG09JnBtPWJsb2cmb2Zmc2V0PTA%3D.

up, makes mistakes and constantly causes trouble for his partner, provoking laughter, setting the pace and winning the audience's affection.[33]

As mentioned above, there are more than 220 comics and stories featuring these detectives, encompassing a wide range of legal implications over a period of 66 years. Some of the most evident references to legal dimensions are presented from both international and domestic perspectives.

Characters: Besides the protagonists of the comics, some of the other main characters are *Superintendente Vicente* (Súper), who is one of the top-ranking officials at T.I.A., ranking just below the General Director. Even as a child, he stood out for his moustache, inherited from his father (the gas delivery man). As the head of the T.I.A. agents, he is the one who assigns missions to Mortadelo and Filemón. These are usually the most difficult missions for several reasons: either he doesn't want to risk the lives of his valuable agents, his best agents aren't available or he simply lacks agents with the necessary skills. He is an authoritarian boss and could even be called a despot due to his methods of 'persuasion' (such as threatening his agents with a hug from Schiffer – a python, for example), or direct aggression and threats. On the other hand, he has also shown to be a good person when things go as they should.[34]

Ofelia Michelínez, a surname that parodies the name *michelín* (spare tyre) by adding the termination 'ez', a patronymic suffix, very common in that it indicates descent, meaning 'son of'. She is the secretary of the T.I.A. and her most notable characteristic is her large weight and size. Ofelia always appears delivering the Superintendent's orders to Mortadelo and Filemón. Although she cares for them, she always ends up being humiliated by the two agents. While she is generally a good person, she tends to get angry quickly. She often seeks advice from the other female staff at T.I.A. on how to win over Mortadelo, but the advice always fails because of the agents. She also has conflicts with other women at T.I.A. as they boast about having been asked to be married.[35]

Mortadelo and Filemón's comportment with Ofelia today would be considered politically incorrect and certainly, some expressions and behaviours expressed in the comics have aged badly. The humiliation suffered by the secretary is a clear example of what today would be considered bullying in the workplace. This opens up the debate that has taken place with other works and comics, where elements have been revised to avoid causing offence, such

33 Ibid.

34 'Superintendente Vicente', Mortadelo Wiki, https://mortadelo.fandom.com/es/wiki/Superintendente_Vicente.

35 'Ofelia', Mortadelo Wiki, https://mortadelo.fandom.com/es/wiki/Ofelia.

as in Snow White and the Seven Dwarfs, where the dwarfs are now, for good reason, animals; sections of Roald Dahl books have been rewritten to remove language deemed offensive;[36] and then there is the accusation of racism in Tintin. [37]

Finally, Professor Saturnino Bacterio is a scientist at T.I.A. Although he has shown knowledge in nearly every possible field, his inventions have mostly failed. He hired Mortadelo as an assistant to test a hair tonic, which left him bald. Mortadelo lost his hair, his patience and his job, while Professor Bacterio lost his teeth (although in some episodes, he is shown to still have a good set of teeth, which he hides with his beard). He typically uses Mortadelo and Filemón to test his inventions, leading to several albums dedicated to his creations.[38]

The adversaries in these stories vary widely. Typically, they consist of organised criminals or masterminds with treacherous schemes that could pose a global threat. However, in some instances, the 'enemies' are not traditional villains at all but rather a reflection of the absurd and chaotic situations Mortadelo and Filemón often find themselves in. During the early stages, there were even scenarios where no true enemies existed, with the humour and conflict arising more from the agents' own incompetence or mishaps. On rare occasions, the antagonists are extraterrestrial beings or superhuman entities, including Bacterio's failed inventions, which often result in bizarre and unpredictable challenges for the duo.[39]

Structure of the plot: In Mortadelo and Filemón comics, there are a series of recurring elements that structure the plot: (a) There is a secret entrance which is usually an everyday object: a fountain, a sign or a tree. These entrances often cause them problems, like tight spaces and various forms of dirtiness. But it's even worse for passersby who try to use them, only to find that they're just normal objects for anyone who isn't an agent of T.I.A.; (b) Mortadelo and Filemón try, unsuccessfully, to avoid their responsibilities. They often

36 H. Vernon, 'Roald Dahl books rewritten to remove language deemed offensive', The Guardian, 18 February 2023, https://www.theguardian.com/books/2023/feb/18/roald-dahl-books-rewritten-to-remove-language-deemed-offensive.

37 'British political correctness goes a step too far, branding Tintin racist', La Stampa, 5 November 2011, https://www.lastampa.it/vatican-insider/en/2011/11/05/news/british-political-correctness-goes-a-step-too-far-branding-tintin-racist-1.36917787/#google_vignette.

38 'Profesor Bacterio', Mortadelo Wiki, https://mortadelo.fandom.com/es/wiki/Profesor_Bacterio.

39 Y. García, 'Los 13 mejores villanos de Mortadelo y Filemón', Cinemanía, 25 November 2014, https://www.20minutos.es/cinemania/noticias/los-13-mejores-villanos-de-mortadelo-y-filemon-27632/.

pretend to be sick or flee to distant places, only to be picked up by another agent from T.I.A. This happens when they are faced with particularly dangerous missions; (c) Professor Bacterio's inventions never work as they should. This well-meaning but inaccurate version of James Bond's Q often gives them gadgets or potions that have the opposite of the intended effect; (d) The means of transport assigned to them by T.I.A. always disappoint; (e) Mortadelo uses disguises to escape his bosses. He uses his disguises more often to evade hammers or escape from Súper or Filemón than to carry out missions. Sometimes, the disguise is impractical for escaping and is more related to the weapon being used against him, though he often resorts to a turtle shell disguise; and (f) When they try to protect someone, things get worse.[40]

No matter what they do, the person they are protecting ends up in more danger and everything ends badly. Even if they solve the case, Mortadelo and Filemón often end their adventures (and each chapter) running away from the Súper, who wants revenge for their latest blunder, which usually leaves him bandaged or scorched.[41]

Comics Representing Domestic and International Legal Aspects

Mortadelo and Filemón comics deal in some cases expressly with legal and political topics. Therefore, there is no need for overly forced or experimental interpretations to observe the legal issues and the sarcastic, humorous critique of the specific subject of the comic. In other stories, the reference is more veiled, but it is easy to interpret what or who it is in fact referring to.

Following the proposed structure, the following highlight some comics with international plots. The first comic to mention is:

a) *El sulfato atómico* (The Atomic Sulphate), from 27 January to 30 June 1969, is the first long story written about Mortadelo and Filemón and features Professor Bacterio for the first time. It is perhaps the comic that took Ibáñez the longest to complete; he once mentioned that it took him three times as long as he usually spent on each page. This is because this comic contains some of the most intricate work in each panel, due to the level of detail in every background and composition.[42]

---

40 J. Rubio Hancock, '11 escenas que pasan en todas las historietas de Mortadelo y Filemón'.

41 Ibid.

42 A. Santaliestra, 'El Sulfato Atómico: el salto cualitativo de Mortadelo y Filemón', Cuántica Gáfica, 16 July 2023, https://cuanticagrafica.com/2023/07/16/el-sulfato-atomico-el-salto-cualitativo-de-mortadelo-y-filemon/.

El sulfato atómico marked a turning point in Ibáñez's career. He now played in the big leagues and exhibited a clear Franco-Belgian influence: from Professor Bacterio (who bears a resemblance to 'Professor Zwart', a secondary character from *Spirou* that appeared in *The Mine and the Gorilla* in 1956) to the initial premise, which draws varying degrees of inspiration from *The Case of the Three-Fingered Glove* (1965) by Tillieux and *The Calculus Affair* (1956) by Hergé.[43]

The plot starts with the creation of a lotion, 'atomic sulphate', by Professor Bacterio, which, according to him, eliminates crop pests. However, the lotion has the exact opposite effect: it significantly enlarges animals, making it a severe threat to humanity. The worst part of the situation is that one of the bottles containing the compound was stolen by agents of the Republic of Tyranny. There, the dictator Bruteztrausen rules and he plans to use it to dominate the world. Mortadelo and Filemón's mission is to go to Tyranny and retrieve the bottle. However, the border agents expel them because Mortadelo, by mistake, grabbed recipe books instead of passports. As a result, they must enter in disguise, using Mortadelo's costumes. They reach the city, manage to enter the palace, snatch the bottle from right under the president's nose and escape, all thanks to a bottle of that very sulphate that they brought from Spain.[44] The comic was written during the Francoist dictatorship, and the characters fly to a fascist fictional dictatorship. More than 50 years since its publication, *El Sulfato Atómico* is an icon and a masterpiece of comic art, that is internationally recognised.

b) *Maastricht... Jesús!* [Maastricht... Jesus!] of 27 January 1993, has a title that plays on the similarity between the word 'Maastricht' (when read in Spanish) and the onomatopoeia 'Achís', which refers to a sneeze. This is why it continues with the word *Jesús*, which is commonly said in Spanish to invoke divine protection and ward off contagion.

This story satirises the Maastricht Treaty, which was crucial for the creation of the European Union. In the plot, Mortadelo and Filemón must protect the candidates vying to become president of the 'United Europe'. The comic includes many references to real European political figures of the time, such as Felipe González, Helmut Kohl, Jacques Chirac, Giulio Andreotti,

43 Ibid.

44 'The Atomic Sulphate and Magin the Magician', Instituto Cervantes, https://cultura.cervantes.es/sidney/en/el-sulfato-atómico-y-magin-el-mago/122313.

John Major and Jean-Luc Dehaene, though their names are altered to add a humorous touch.[45]

The gag that opens each chapter is a typical slapstick routine in Mortadelo and Filemón: Filemón hears that Mortadelo is trying on a disguise and charges at him, but it's Filemón who ends up taking the hit. This is followed by the arrival of a message from El Súper, which also results in a blow to Filemón or some other misfortune. Additionally, in each chapter, they must use one of the famous secret entrances to T.I.A.[46]

In the final chapter, the two agents search for the secret entrance to T.I.A. in an underground maze. On their first attempt, Filemón ends up in Queen Isabel II's bathtub. After swimming across the English Channel, they try again. When Mortadelo opens the hatch, boiling water spills onto Filemón. Mortadelo peeks in and finds himself in a cauldron in hell, surrounded by two demons; inside the cauldron is Francisco Franco.[47]

c) *Llegó el Euro* (The Euro has arrived) is a comic of 25 October 2001, where Helmut Kohl, during a high-profile meeting of European leaders, including Spain's Felipe González, proposes the adoption of the German mark as the single currency for the European Union. This moment reflects the debates and negotiations surrounding the creation of a unified European currency, which would later become the euro. A series of counterfeit euro bills is spreading across Europe. Súper assigns Mortadelo and Filemón to find out who the counterfeiter is, basing their investigation on clues found in the images on the fake bills.[48]

Mortadelo and Filemón are tasked with following a series of clues found in the images printed on the fake bills. These visual hints are scattered across various Countries, taking the duo on an international chase. Their first destination is Japan, where they suspect a man named Kemato Tagüela might be involved. To assist in their investigation, they enlist the help of Sakudo Kastaña, a formidable sumo wrestler.[49] Both names are comical since, in Spanish they mean 'I killed your grandmother' and 'I shake a chestnut', which refers to striking something.

45 Segonaocasio, 'Mortadelo y Filemon Maastricht Jesus', TodoColeccion, https://www.todocoleccion.net/tebeos-bruguera/mortadelo-filemon-maastricht-jesus~x500789782.

46 F. J. de la Cruz Pérez, *Los cómics de Francisco Ibáñez*, (Cuenca: Ediciones de la UCLM, 2008).

47 M. Fernández Soto, *El mundo de Mortadelo y Filemón* (Palma de Mallorca: Dolmen Editorial. Colección Storyteller, 2015).

48 'Maastricht…¡Jesús!', La Página no Oficial de Mortadelo y Filemón, https://mortadelo-filemon.es/ficha_content?q=YWlkPTE1Nzc%3D.

49 'Llego el Euro', Mortadelo Wiki, https://mortadelo.fandom.com/es/wiki/Llegó_el_euro.

With his unique strength and knowledge of the local area, Sakudo becomes an unlikely ally as Mortadelo and Filemón navigate the complexities of Japanese culture and encounter slapstick misadventures. From Japan, their mission takes them across the globe to the United States, where they follow more leads and experience the typical chaos that accompanies their investigations. However, despite their journey through major world powers, the surprising twist comes when they finally track down the elusive counterfeiter, not in a major financial centre, but in a small, inconspicuous village in Spain.[50]

This humorous and adventurous storyline blends real political figures and events with the absurdity and charm of Mortadelo and Filemón's world. It captures both the tension of the debates over the European currency and the playful satire that characterises their comic adventures, as they bumble their way through an international conspiracy while poking fun at contemporary figures and global politics.[51]

d) *Drones Matones* (bully drones) of 5 July 2017. New technologies have also arrived at T.I.A., so Mortadelo and Filemón need to get up to speed. Professor Bacterio has created a drone to assist the agents in their missions and to locate other drones that may cause problems, destroying them in the process. With this new gadget from Bacterio, Mortadelo and Filemón will embark on one of their most outrageous adventures.[52] The new technology is presented to the president of the *Estados Juntitos*, a humorous name for the United States, President Donald Trompf, while Mortadelo disguises himself as Donald Duck.

In *Drones Matones*, the latest mission that T.I.A. has set out on is to eliminate all traces of spy drones using an invention from Professor Bacterio. This service could be of great interest to the United States and President Trompf, especially since they are so concerned about interference from foreign Countries. However, the blunders of the bumbling Carpetovetonic spies will not fully convince Trompf, who will complain several times about the agents' shoddy work. In one of those instances, they lose control of the device, which ends up crashing into the head of the blonde president.[53]

e) *Cambio climático* (Climate Change) 13 October 2021. In this adventure of Mortadelo and Filemón, the Súper assigns the T.I.A. agents a mission in

50 Ibid.

51 Ibid.

52 C. Geli, 'Trump recibe un chichón de Mortadelo y Filemón', El País, 2 June 2017, https://elpais.com/ccaa/2017/06/01/catalunya/1496354388_620035.html.

53 'Trump, la última víctima de los torpes 'Mortadelo y Filemón', La Opinión A Coruña, 2 June 2017, https://www.laopinioncoruna.es/cultura/2017/06/02/trump-ultima-victima-torpes-mortadelo-24260267.html.

which they must combat the effects of climate change, which is causing problems all over the planet. The story arrived in bookshops ten days before the celebration of World Climate Change Day, which takes place on 24 October. In this new adventure, the Súper assigns the agents a mission in which they must combat the effects of climate change, which is causing problems all over the planet. With the invaluable help of Professor Bacterio's inventions, they will need to visit the most remote villages in Spain, where the climate has been affected by the significant changes.[54]

The agents make some predictions about what awaits the planet if no action is taken: Santa Claus will trade in his red coat for floral shorts; priests will have to call the faithful to mass by shouting because the church bells will have been blown away by hurricane winds; and the umbrellas on the terraces of bars will disappear to shelter the donkeys that pull the ploughs.[55]

From a domestic perspective, Ibáñez's characters have focused on satirising corruption, real estate slipshods and cutbacks; problems of his contemporary times. An attachment to reality means that there are those who claim (Nacho Carretero) that a certain part of the essence of the characters is lost, as he explained.[56] But it is also undeniable that these stories full of botched jobs and failures are one of the best ways of explaining what is happening in Spain. A clear example of this is the comics that the author has dedicated to the crisis: Ibáñez uses his nonsensical humour as a weapon to denounce (kindly, but accurately) real estate speculation, scams and cutbacks.[57] No one is spared, as political figures of the moment, encompassing the entire parliamentary arc, from Catalan pro-independence politicians to left and right parties are targeted.

In other adventures, our secret agents are involved with the new institution of the popular jury, *El Jurado* (The Jury) of 26 April 1996, coinciding with the approval of the law of the jury in Spain, with the cover already featuring, in a sarcastic way, a rope. In the plot, the Súper instructs Mortadelo and Filemón to guard the popular jury in the trial against Joe Roetráqueas (who gnawed tracheas). The jury is made up of other characters of Ibáñez (*Rompetechos*, the Zoo vet, Grandma Napoleona, the teacher Miss Rufina) and a man in a suit and black shirt, with a hat that covers his eyes, who doesn't speak for most of

---

54 'Mortadelo y Filemón luchan contra el cambio climático en el nuevo cómic de Ibáñez', 20minutos, 13 October 2021, https://www.20minutos.es/noticia/4853323/0/mortadelo-y-filemon-apuestan-por-combatir-el-cambio-climatico-en-su-nuevo-tomo/.

55 Ibid.

56 N. Carretero, 'Mortadelo y Filemón, espejo de España'.

57 J. Rubio Hancock, 'La crisis explicada por Mortadelo y Filemón', Verne, 21 March 2015, https://verne.elpais.com/verne/2015/03/17/articulo/1426605381_635577.html.

the story, but from whose thoughts it can be deduced that he has been linked to delinquency.[58] The agents even founded their own political party, *Elecciones* (Elections), on 4 November 2015 to defeat the *Partido Papilar*, in a clear allusion to the Partido Popular, the quintessential conservative party in Spain.

Conclusion

This chapter starts by justifying something that seems obvious: Ibáñez and his characters are a cultural phenomenon in Spain. This is evident, as one only has to look at the long career, merits and recognitions in life and posthumously that the author and his characters have received. In fact, it can be stated that somehow Mortadelo and Filemón, Rompetechos and the characters of *13 rue del percebe*, have come to life, and are undoubtedly part of our own world. On the other hand, it is complicated to constrain the meaning and significance of this author and his work in Spanish culture. Criticism is necessary in any political system. Whoever manages to do it by making people, children and adults, laugh is a brilliant person.

The selection of comics presented in this chapter is a small sample of the legal and political reality that the author has been capturing throughout his long career. I feel that I have not done justice to Ibáñez's immense work. However, I hope to have captured the author's transcendence in our society and to invite the reader of the chapter to delve into his work. Although they are probably a foreign audience, I would recommend comics that deal with international or intergalactic aspects that do not require prior knowledge of the reality and the characters (these are not fictional) of Spanish politics. Some of the cartoons mentioned in this chapter, as well as others featuring Silvio Berlusconi, Angela Merkel, Nicolas Sarkozy, Vladimir Putin, Barack Obama and the late Muammar Gaddafi, which have been the subject of Ibáñez's pen and pencil, are surely a good starting point for foreign readers to understand the author's approach.

Criticism, however acidic and sarcastic it may appear, is not offensive, neither in its form nor in its substance, and proof of this is that there are no lawsuits or quarrels against Ibáñez, and any person of any ideology has laughed at his comics; it has become a phenomenon that transcends the cultural sphere. In fact, it can be taken as a shining example, at a time when political polarisation and lack of dialogue between adversaries is the general rule in Spain and other European Countries, where the adversary has become the enemy to be

58 'El Jurado Popular', Mortadelo y Filemón Wiki, https://mortadelo-y-filemn.fandom.com/es/wiki/El_jurado_popular.

beaten at any cost. Surely, and accidentally, Mortadelo and Filemón could have avoided some sad episodes in their Country and in Europe and the rest of the world.

I believe that there is no better way to conclude this chapter than stating the sentence that Pilar Diago sent to me in an email: *¡Larga vida a Mortadelo y Filemón!* (Long live Mortadelo and Filemón!).

Chapter 8

'BEST CLOSER BEYOND RULES' BETWEEN LEGAL DRAMA AND CONTEMPORARY PUBLIC ETHICS IN SUITS: POP CULTURE THEORY VS. LEGAL CULTURE?

Giovanna Tieghi

The Comparatist 'Traveler' and Suits: Introductory Reflections on Method and Content

The idea of pushing the gaze beyond the traditional boundaries of comparative law to try to understand the scope and implications of the 'representation of legal traditions in pop culture' has a specific, twofold meaning: it is not only a demonstration of the importance, for the jurist, of tapping into the 'marketplace of ideas'[1] referred to in the historical lesson of the Canadian Supreme Court, as well as its implications for the method *in* and *of* comparative law.

1 These are the words of the Supreme Court of Canada on the occasion of the Reference re *Secession of Quebec (1998) 2 S.C.R.*, evoked also with reference to the importance of 'the contribution of ideas and reflections on issues and problems of the moment'. Precisely in order to stimulate dialogue and dialectical confrontation, it has been recalled that the *Reference* sealed a historical moment by declaring that 'the proper functioning of a democracy requires a permanent process of discussion': indeed, as the Court emphasized, 'no one has a monopoly on the truth' and 'the best solutions' must be sought in the 'marketplace of ideas.' M. Bertolissi, 'Presentazione', in *Giornata di studi in ricordo di Livio Paladin. Riforme, Opinioni a confronto,* M. Bertolissi (Napoli: Jovene, 2015): VII-VIII. The premise? The 'continuous process of discussion and evolution' of democratic institutions, which, transposed into the contribution that the academy can make to the understanding of new realities that intersect with the legal tradition, translates into the 'reciprocal obligation on the other participants to engage in discussion'. In this case, 'to address any legitimate initiative to change the constitutional order', item No. 150 of the above-mentioned *Reference.* In the case of the Study Conference, to 'push the analysis down to the level of values', thus to the consideration of 'living law systems' as the proper purpose of the comparative method

It is, above all, the avant-garde inversion of the role of the contemporary comparatist: who is, or must be, par excellence, a real 'traveller of the theory and practice of the legal universe'.[2] And furthermore, not only of the legal universe, but of everything that, in terms of interdisciplinarity,[3] can serve as a 'shortcut to understanding the world'.[4] Thus, also 'beyond law'.[5]

'Life is like this' (in the scene, the main character indicates one level with his hand); 'I like it like this' (indicating a much higher level).[6] 'I don't have dreams, I have goals'. These cult phrases delineate the thread of the interaction between pop culture and legal culture. For their scenic-argumentative power, some other expressions will be used[7] to qualify the eclecticism and ambition of the protagonist of the New York lawyer Harvey Specter, thus capturing the same interaction in terms of method and law in action. What influence does pop culture have today, and how much does it contribute to the understanding of a legal system[8] and of profession practicing in that area? How much does the televised representation of the cultural identity of this profession influence public opinion? What is the impact of pop culture on the global practice of professional law? Which practices – or expressions – of behaviour reproduced in the legal drama contribute – do or do not contribute – to a more realistic understanding of the role of the lawyer as the nexus of the network of actors operating in the legal field? To what extent does Specter's murderous, edgy and ruthless attitude represent the ideal of professional acuity and success, and to what extent do his relationships (with clients and with

---

(translation by the author): G. Bognetti, 'L'oggetto e il metodo', in *Diritto costituzionale comparato,* eds. P. Carrozza, A. Di Giovine and G.F. Ferrari, Tomo II (Roma-Bari: Laterza, 2014): 728.

2 T.E. Frosini, *Diritto pubblico comparato. Le democrazie stabilizzate* (Bologna: il Mulino, 2022): 18.

3 And, in particular, here, in the 'Law and [...]' perspective (see P.G. Monateri, 'Forward: "Law &..."', *DPCE*, no. 2 (2021)), with reference to linguistics and argumentation science studies: on the topic, G. Tieghi, '"Looking Beyond our Borders". A Challenging Legal Linguistic Journey Through the New Directions of Comparative Law', in *Comparative Law and Global English for Legal Studies. A Law-Linguistic Journey*, ed. G. Tieghi (Napoli: Jovene, 2024).

4 'Chapter I. The comparative method: shortcut to understanding the world' (translation by the author): L. Pegoraro, A. Rinella, *Sistemi costituzionali comparati* (Torino: Giappichelli, 2017). For an in-depth discussion on 'Rereading and reaffirming "comparative law" for the effectiveness of contemporary law': G. Tieghi, 'Educare, non solo decidere. Nuovi scenari dalle recenti opere dei giudici costituzionali Grossi e Sotomayor', *Rivista AIC*, no. 1 (2020): from 177.

5 L. Pegoraro, A. Rinella, *Sistemi costituzionali comparati,* quot.: from 18.

6 The stage performance of which can be seen at https://www.youtube.com/watch?v=IRq6pS2pv5Y (from 1:39).

7 The original language (English) is helpful so as not to compromise the strength of its authenticity: found in https://collider.com/suits-harvey-specter-quotes-ranked/.

8 G. Martinico, 'Lamps and Mirrors: Studying Law Through Pop Culture', in *Comparative Law and Global English for Legal Studies. A Law-Linguistic Journey*, ed. G. Tieghi, quot.: from 93.

his associate Mike Ross – young and enterprising, but whose professional profile is based on a lie) reveal the need for a scientific study of the dichotomy between legal culture and pop culture?[9]

In the light of the double value of the term, wisely chosen by the authors of the television series as the title of the programme, such questions take on particular significance also in the sense of stimulating the jurist to a critical attitude in a global perspective.[10] *Suits*, in fact, is not only, as a matter of law, 'any proceeding by one or more parties against another in a court of law – also termed a lawsuit'[11] – which, among other things, originally distinguished 'a suit in equity as opposed to an action at law'.[12] In the common English lexicon, it is also a specific item of clothing (which, not surprisingly, correlates with the law firm environment): the suit – or suit for women.

In a broader legal-linguistic perspective – especially in its verbal form – that word refers to something that is well suited, that fits well, that is appropriate: for this physique, for the place, ultimately, also for the circumstances. Just like the legal ideal, which is always to be sought, in a continuous process, so that it best fits the context, the concrete case, the 'constitutional dimension of coexistence',[13] the identity of a system:[14] 'Law in context',[15] the motto for the study of law and society. It is a teaching that takes on a significant meaning in this context. It is the one that relates to the perspective of the link between rights and obligations.[16] Just like the suit: 'People notice what we wear', is one of Specter's lessons to his trainee. 'Put on your tuxedo, we're

9 R. K. Sherwin, *When Law Goes Pop: The Vanishing Line Between Law and Popular Culture* (Chicago: Chicago University Press, 2000).

10 So as to foster a 'comparative study [...] which, leaving behind the rigid schematism of legal systems theory [...] tends to take root in the concrete of legal experiences as a ground for sharing common problems and needs' (translation by the author): L. Moccia, 'Comparazione giuridica, diritto e giurista europeo: un punto di vista globale', in *Alessandro Giuliani: l'esperienza giuridica fra logica ed etica*, eds. F. Cerrone and G. Repetto (Milan: Giuffrè, 2012), vol. 95: 258.

11 *Black's Law Dictionary*, Bryan A. Garner (Editor-in-Chief) (Eagan: West Publishing Co., 1996): 605.

12 *Oxford Dictionary of Law* (Oxford: Oxford University Press, 2015): 604.

13 P. Grossi, *Relazione del Presidente Paolo Grossi sulla giurisprudenza costituzionale del 2015*, in https://www.cortecostituzionale.it/documenti/interventi_presidente/RelazioneGrossi2015.pdf: 2.

14 G. Capograssi, 'Analisi dell'esperienza comune', in *Opere*, ed. M. D'Addio and E. Vidal (Milano: Giuffrè, 1959), vol. II; A. D'Auria, *La scienza giuridica come sistema vitale in Giuseppe Capograssi* (Napoli: Editoriale Scientifica, 2008).

15 'A contextual approach involves treating legal subjects broadly, using materials from other humanities and social sciences, and from any other disciplines that help to explain the operation in practice of the particular legal field or legal phenomena under investigation': 'About Law in Context', *Law in Context Series*, Cambridge, in www.cambridge.org.

16 For a discussion of the concept of 'fidelity to context', see P. Selznick, '"Law in Context" Revisited', *Journal of Law and Society*, 30, no. 2 (2003).

busy'; 'The better you dress, the worse you can behave'. Form over substance or, rather, a more up-to-date reading of contemporary cultural – including legal – reality?[17]

Pop culture and legal culture theories put to the test of contemporaneity

If the terrain of facts is 'the typical terrain of history',[18] and therefore also of contemporaneity, it is crucial to take, as the perspective of investigation, the one that, taking note of the intersection between the two cultural theories (pop and legal), best contributes to the outlining of new scenarios – useful, above all, for understanding and decoding reality. In short, to orient empirically – aware of the crisis at hand.[19] It is the concept of legal culture[20] as a 'network' – that is, as a crossroads with other sciences or arts – 'of values and attitudes relating to law, which determines when and why and where people turn to law or government or turn away'.[21]

---

17 The 'world of facts – natural, economic, social', it has been authoritatively reminded, 'is not the inert and sterile terrain of mere legal irrelevance, as preached by the scheme of the statist and legalist voluntarism of the "moderns", delivering into the hands of a legislator/demurge the power to convert (in its libito) into law a reality conceived as a merely magmatic heap; the world of facts is, instead, the typical terrain of history' (translation by the author): P. Grossi, *L'invenzione del diritto* (Roma-Bari: Laterza, 2017), part on *L'invenzione della Costituzione: l'esperienza italiana*: 69.

18 See footnote 15.

19 ' it's not for nothing that we speak of a "crisis", which, as I often reply, is not a crisis of law, but a crisis of the way in which we have tried to nail down (and reduce) its sources. [...] Whether we like it or not, the axis of the legal system has shifted, and since this is a real fact before our eyes, we simply have to take note of it. The historian of law – attentive to the dialectic between the past and the present, marked by a line that is eloquent to the attentive eye – has realized, and not only today, the significance of this line, all of which is aimed at valuing interpreters/inventors, whether theoreticians or practitioners, in the grace of their pliability. Judges, academics, lawyers, and notaries can guarantee a legal response that is truly capable of ordering the transition. In short, this is the current legal situation, and it is common wise not to attempt an inefficient removal, deceived by dazzling mythologies' (translation by the author): P. Grossi, *Il diritto in una società che cambia. A colloquio con Orlando Roselli* (Bologna: il Mulino, 2018): 112, in Chapter III, more precisely entitled, 'The Challenges of Contemporary Societies. The contribution of legal thought for a law in keeping with the times': 107. Among other things, it is worth mentioning that ' today, as yesterday, it is not a crisis of the law but a crisis of its historically dated conception': in O. Roselli, 'Uno storico del diritto alla Corte costituzionale', in P. Grossi, *Il diritto in una società che cambia*, quot.: 10.

20 G. Samuel, 'What is the Impact of Culture on Legal Theory'? *Droit et Société*, no. 1 (2019), n. 101, referring to R. Provost (ed.), *Cultures in the Domains of Law* (Cambridge: Cambridge University Press, 2017).

21 This is the definition first coined by Lawrence Friedman in his article 'Legal Culture and Social Development', *Law & Society Review*, no. 4 (1969).

The question arises, then, precisely with reference to the protagonist (H.S.), who would operate, as proposed in the pop perspective – that is, for the purpose of constituting images of individuals and groups, their identity, their way of lifestyle within the contemporary 'mass' cultural reality – 'beyond rules': 'truth and non-truth of the popular'?[22]

Friedman's values approach, which has been put forward since the early 1970s as a challenge to the understanding of the 'explanatory power' of the concept of legal culture, allows us to extend the investigation from a theoretical to an empirical level, with a specific focus on one group of professionals: lawyers. This includes the attempt – typical of pop culture – to convey the 'basic understanding of law' to the public through so-called cultural products, including television series.[23] In relation to lawyers in particular, legal culture – here in its sense of a 'mixture of genres' – should therefore be measured by certain indices (i.e. 'five attitudinal components') such as: 'general legitimacy and acceptance of authority, legitimacy of norms for dispute resolution, procedural preferences, objectives of dispute resolution and discretion and particularism in legal decisions'.[24]

It is not, as it might appear, a division between so-called high ('high' or 'serious' culture) and low ('low' or 'popular') culture; it is the multidimensional meaning of popular culture that imposes itself – as is precisely the case in the contemporary era, including the legal sphere and its law in action[25] – as a prism for a critical understanding of the era we live in. Being, or appearing? Truth, or lies? 'It's not bragging if it's true', one of Specter's famous phrases. And, 'He who wins, gives no credit to the ball, the basket or the wind speed in the room'.

Ambition, Success, Relationships: 'Relational' Law Between Legal Drama and Reality

In the most avant-garde studies on the subject, the legal culture of professionals places the lawyer at stake and, above all, his professionalism 'in

22 It is also the title of an essay that is a critique of contemporary society but has direct implications as a critique of how that society is represented, even on television: S. Marino, *Verità e non-verità del popular. Saggio su Adorno, dimensione estetica e critica della società* (Milano: Mimesis, 2021).
23 M. Asomow, K. Brown, D. R. Papke (eds.), *Law and Popular Culture. International Perspectives* (Cambridge: Cambridge Scholars Publishing, 2014).
24 G. Bierbrauer, 'Toward an Understanding of Legal Culture: Variations in Individualism and Collectivism between Kurds, Lebanese, and Germans', *Law & Society Review*, no. 28 (1994): 248.
25 *Culture and Law in action*, in G. Samuel, 'What is the Impact of Culture on Legal Theory?', quot., 2.

performing tasks related to law and the legal system'. Thus are represented 'attitudes and values of legal practitioners'[26] according to Friedman's sense of values. For some authors, however, there is something more: it is the 'professional sensibility, habits of mind and intellectual reflexes';[27] what is the role, in all of this, of the sense of ambition – up to and including unbridled ambition – that characterizes the everyday life of Attorney Specter, hungry for success and obsessed with winning? What is the value that, according to the notion of legal culture expounded here, really 'affects the relationship between law in books and law in practice'?[28]

The representation of the role of the lawyer in the Suits series can be defined by an evaluative analysis that, while having an immediate impact on the audience and the collective imagination, also says a lot about the skills that the lawyer (not the actor/lawyer) must have in today's society. Qualities which are in place for a dual purpose. Firstly, technical skills and behavioural strategies to operate in complex legal systems, where the complexity of experience is increasingly presented as the result of a network of relationships. Instead of becoming a trap, the latter must be seen as a challenge to expand the potential of the individual, including his or her human weaknesses (para. 2). Secondly, professional and human qualities that need to be adapted to the present day in order to redefine the profession itself in a process of re-education. The latter requires behavioural, linguistic and, above all, professional preparation and competence, all of which are needed today more than ever in order to respond to contemporary demands for justice (para. 3). Vocational training must be essentially an expression of culture.[29]

As for the first aspect, two key words mark the evaluative path of the representation of the legal tradition in the *Suits* series. This is illustrated by some of the protagonist's cult phrases:

26 E. Zimmermann, 'Legal Culture and State Building: Liberal Constitutionalism and Droit Administratif in early Twentieth Century Argentina', *Int. Jour. For the Semiotics of Law* (2016).

27 M. Hunt, 'The Human Rights Act and Legal Culture: The Judiciary and the Legal Profession', *Journal of Law and Society* (1999): 87.

28 M. Cehulic, 'Perspectives of Legal Culture: A Systematic Literature Review', *Revija za Sociologiju*, vol. 51, no. 2 (2021): 260.

29 On the subject, in particular, P. Grossi, 'Nobiltà culturale degli avvocati', *Rassegna Forense*, no. 1 (2011). In the same direction: G. Bergonzini, L. Locatelli, G. Tieghi (eds.), *Etica, deontologia e tecnica dell'avvocato. Nuove sfide alla prova della contemporaneità* (Giuffrè, Milano, 2023). The volume, which is first and foremost a cultural operation, collects the writings of all the professors, practitioners and professionals who work as lecturers in the various teaching modules, and in particular that of forensic deontology, within the School of Forensic Training of the Padua Bar Association.

(a) 'Ambition' is also based on a good dose of narcissism and self-centredness, to the point of conveying the belief – especially of the protagonist – that at the basis of success there must always be an indispensable prerequisite: charisma and self-confidence. 'Anyone can do my job, but no one can be me'; 'Sorry, I can't hear you over the sound of how great I am'; 'I don't get lucky. I make my own luck'.
(b) 'Success': 'That's the difference between you and me. You want to lose small. I want to win big'; 'He's the best lawyer after me'; 'No one has ever turned me down'; 'For me it's 0 to 2, and 0 is not the number that's going to change'; 'I play to win'

Contrary to what it might appear, the two attitudes, through the ruthless cynicism of attorney Harvey Specter, reveal not only the appeal of the protagonist's individual personality but, more importantly, the relationships over which he presides. Thus, through his character, he shows how human events affect the way the profession is practised. In fact, these relationships intersect his professional skills with his human qualities (or, non-qualities) to such an extent that the portrayal goes far beyond the legal drama, *Suits*. This is precisely because of his relationship with the smart young associate. 'Let's make one thing be clear: I'm not Charlie Brown, you're not Lucy'; 'Because Butch was the boss and Sundance was the gunslinger, and I'm both'. These are the metaphors that represent them and that become part of their language. They help transpose their complicity into the world of film almost to portray a different ideal other than the legal one. On the contrary, however, it is the law itself that makes use of this component: 'Law is a relationship with others, sharing part of what you have, commitment and duty. Then it is right'.[30]

The most significant relationship on the pop-legal level is precisely that with his collaborator, Mike Ross. Undermining all interview participants, Mike will quickly become his right-hand man ('If you want to know how to be a lawyer, I'm your man, but if you want advice on love, I don't know what to tell you') although he does not hold all the cards and for whom Specter, never ready to express his emotions ('I'm against having emotions, not against using them') is ready to do anything to protect him ('Say what

30 M. Bertolissi, *Autonomia e responsabilità sono un punto di vista* (Napoli: Jovene, 2015), cover page. And again, ' law is one of the ways to change the world, because everything can be traced back to the relationship between people, the State and the law' (translation by the author): these are Calabresi's words to the students of Macerata, on the occasion of the *Alberico Gentili Lectures*, Macerata, March 1921 2012: B. Barbisan, *Premessa*, in G. Calabresi, *Il mestiere di giudice. Pensieri di un accademico americano* (Bologna: il Mulino, 2013): 13.

you want, but I don't leave the one I'm partnered with. That's it, it's funny because it's from Top Gun') and teach him the trade ('work until you don't have to introduce yourself'; 'You read books, I read people'). But there is also the relationship with the customer ('Whether right or wrong, no matter who he is, the customer has to be happy!', 'I'm not the guy who hugs you when you're scared. I'm the guy that wins when you need it the most') and, last but not least, with Harvard Ethics Professor Gerard, who will be discovered, thanks to Harvey's legal patronage, to have taken a bribe from a student.[31]

This has to do with the concept of so-called relational law in a version that goes beyond the traditional framework of family law. It has more to do with the art of teaching the craft, of motivating, of encouraging, of knowing, of being able to relate on different levels, and thus, of aiming high to always be up to the task. How high? To what extent? When does fiction become reality?

'You have to be three steps ahead of him, because I assure you, he will be two steps ahead of you'; 'Get it straight in your head, first impressions last. If you start at the back you'll never get to the front'; 'If they hate you, use it to your advantage'; 'The only time success comes before work is in the dictionary'.

The Harvard Admission Challenge: Intersection of social responsibility and symptomatic contemporary events

'Love one another', said Calabresi dean of Yale from 1985 to 1994, in his welcome address to the first-year class; 'love one another, because by loving one another you will become better people, and also better lawyers'.[32] What does it mean, today, to become 'better' lawyers? It all begins in the academic environment. It is there that the lawyers of tomorrow are formed.[33] It is there that not only the identity of the lawyer in action is formed, but also the gap between the two formations: 'This is not school. Don't show me the test, give

---

31 For a reconstruction of the role and entanglements between Prof. Gerard, Harvard and the Pearson study, refer to the *storyline* of events concerning him in *Suits*, at https://suits.blogfree.net/?t=5762635.

32 B. Barbisan, *Premessa*, quot., 12.

33 'Too often in universities we narrate a law that is not there. [...] We do not understand the reason why we are silent, or almost silent, about the real contexts in which they (i.e. the legal systems) are placed and by which they often end up being overwhelmed' (translation by the author): U. Vincenti, *Diritto e menzogna. La questione della giustizia in Italia* (Roma: Donzelli, 2013).

me the answer!'; 'In school you're given the lesson. Then the test. In life you're given the test, then the lesson' (Specter to Mike).

In *Suits*, Harvard University – not just any university – is symbolically the place where the events of 'institutional disloyalty'[34] are concentrated. Events that provoke the reaction of the collective imagination and tend to make the pop transposition coincide with the generalised distrust of a category – that of jurists, in general, but also of university professors and lawyers, in particular – traditionally considered, especially the latter, to be mostly amoral. For Mike, the admissions process, known worldwide for its competitiveness, is the Achilles' heel. Mike is the second most important male character in the TV series, which helps to show the fascinating chemistry between him and Harvey. Orphaned by his parents who died in an accident and raised by his grandmother, although a potential candidate for Harvard, Mike will never be able to apply for admission to that university as he had helped a female student by selling her the test results he was able to discover thanks to his photographic memory. She later turned out to be the dean's daughter, and the dean was then forced to resign after the incident. In reality, the sale had been made by his friend Trevor, whom Mike did not want to prejudice by taking responsibility for the event. But the episode – and the report by the dean so that he could never be admitted to that university – marks his life: he will earn his living by getting paid to take the famous 'LSAT' test on behalf of others. And so it is that, still by pure chance, escaping due to an unforeseen contingency related to his friend's shady business dealings, he finds himself in a room used for the selection of candidates for Pearson Hardman, one of the most prestigious law firms in New York. There, he will attract the attention of Attorney Specter, who will choose him as his associate even though he does not meet the primary selection criterion: a law degree, and from Harvard. A profile that Specter himself will hide from the firm's two principals, allowing the candidate's abilities to prevail.

Lies, subterfuge and constant tricks of not revealing the 'secret' intertwine with the everyday cases and relationships that Harvey and Mike have to deal with, always together, getting to know each other day by day, with the incessant pace of work in a law firm and the legal events, never accidental, that reveal the issues of contemporary society, mixing real life with the fascination of dialectics and the often 'tragic' choices of social responsibility. For

---

34 ' one cannot be in societas and enjoy all the benefits that come from this participation without giving something in return or trying to give (*mala maiora vitanda*) as little as possible' (translation by the author): U. Vincenti, 'Etica della giustizia, etica della retribuzione (in margine ad alcune opere di Hogart, Giotto and Lorenzetti)', *Rivista Etica e Filosofia Politica*, no. 14, vol. 2 (2011): 3.

everything revolves around the increasingly untenable lie of the Harvard degree and the paradox of having brilliantly performed on the admission test for others. Ultimately, this is covered up by his superior.

It is no coincidence that the issue is on the international agenda, not least because of its implications for law and constitutional justice. In the first sense, Harvard has been at the centre of debate, including constitutional debate, precisely because of its historic admissions tests. The Supreme Court decided to take up the case, along with that of the University of North Carolina,[35] over allegedly excessive favouritism of black, Hispanic and native American students. The divided Supreme Court struck down affirmative action in college admissions, forcing institutions of higher education to find new ways to achieve diverse student bodies, and declaring that race could not be used.[36] As for profiles more closely related to constitutional justice, the affair even called into question the role of the newly appointed Associate Justice K. B. Jackson and her eventual recusal.[37] Once again ethics, deontology and law collide.

On the Cultural and Ethical Enhancement of Contemporary Lawyering: Focus on Extrajudicial Legal Aid Activity

How much does Suits contribute to the necessary cultural and ethical re-education of contemporary lawyering, given what has already been emphasized? How much, instead, goes in the opposite direction suggesting – at least

35 At issue were 'race-conscious' programs and doubts about their constitutional legitimacy as well as affirmative action initiatives. Both cases were brought by Students for Fair Admissions: C. Walsh, *Supreme Court to hear Harvard admissions challenge*, in *The Harvard Gazette*, at www.news.harvard.edu, 24 January 2022. For the University of North Carolina, see https://www.supremecourt.gov/qp/21-00707qp.pdf. For Harvard University, see https://www.supremecourt.gov/qp/20-01199qp.pdf.

36 *Students for Fair Admissions v. Harvard*, 600 U.S. 181 (2023), was a landmark decision of the Supreme Court of the United States in which the Court held that race-based affirmative action programmes in college admissions processes (excluding military academies) violated the Equal Protection Clause of the Fourteenth Amendment. With its companion case, *Students for Fair Admissions v. University of North Carolina*, the Supreme Court effectively overruled *Grutter v. Bollinger* (2003) and *Regents of the University of California v. Bakke* (1978), which had upheld some affirmative actions in college admissions and provided that race played a limited role in the decisions. See the decision at https://www.supremecourt.gov/opinions/22pdf/20-1199_hgdj.pdf.

37 A. Lancester, 'What would happen if Judge Ketanji Brown Jackson Recused herself in SCOTUS Harvard Admissions Challenge?' 1 April 2022, at https://www.law.com/newyorklawjournal/2022/04/01/what-would-happen-if-judge-ketanji-brown-jackson-recused-herself-in-scotus-harvard-admissions-challenge/.

on the surface – extreme egocentrism, ruthlessness, lack of humanity and cynicism? To what extent is the Specter lawyer the role model for a category that, now more than ever, is clearly using pop culture for an indispensable 'rehabilitation' in the eyes of public opinion? To what extent, on the other hand, is it pop culture that exposes its nefariousness or disloyalty, human before professional?

It is no longer enough *to be* a lawyer. It is imperative *to be one.*[38] Therein lies the difference.'I don't throw gasoline on a pile of matches just to see what happens'. And most importantly, 'Never destroy someone in public if you can achieve the same result in private'.

Leaving aside the minor cases in which Specter refers to the judge as the legal representative in charge of judicial legal aid activities, it is worth dwelling on his approach to extrajudicial legal aid activities and, in particular, to the use of the Alternative Dispute Resolution System (ADRS), where it is the lawyer's soul that proves decisive for 'the last act of a performance'.[39] It is undeniable that his attitude, his courage, even his charm come to the fore and, at the same time, some traits of human frailty and weakness. Profiles of ethics in business?

Law and argumentation: 'Best Closer Beyond Rules'

'Having always some jokes ready' is, in the collective imagination, the idealised representation of the figure of the lawyer; it conveys serenity, security and protection. Not surprisingly, the technique and the theory of argumentation have marked the centuries and are now raising new, significant questions,[40] in particular, studies on the 'alternation between fixity (law) and flexibility (argumentation) in the process of identifying the legal rule'[41] are of particular relevance for an effective analysis of the actions of lawyers belonging to a civil law system.

38 'Re-evaluating lawyers in the representation that the collective imagination has of them is a complicated operation; and yet indispensable, because, as history teaches us, a respected and responsible advocacy is a formidable resource for the proper becoming of law and institutions in general' (translation by the author): A. Mariani Marini, *Agli antipodi dell'azzeccagarbugli. Cultura ed etica dell'avvocato* (Napoli: Jovene, 2009), cover page.

39 Closer, noun, in www.grammar.com.

40 On the problems of *ius dicere* through the method of legal comparison: C. A. D'Alessandro and C. Marchese (eds.), *Ius dicere in a globalized world. A comparative overview* (Rome: RomaTrE-Press, 2018).

41 These are, in particular, those belonging to the Law and Argumentation Laboratory in Padua, a laboratory for legal methodology that also offers many insights from a comparative perspective.

In this context, Harvey assumes the role of closer of negotiation ('Knowledge is knowing what to say. Wisdom is knowing when to say it'). He reveals himself to the audience as the best in New York City, the only one able to combine in his person all the argumentative, strategic and emotional skills of interaction with the other party in order to always come out as the winner, despite the difficulties ('I don't take meetings, I set them and my respect isn't demanded, it's earned'). Dialectical skills, but also strategic skills 'to close a case', to solve a problem possibly before a third party (the judge) decides. The skills required are no less than those required for the role of the person in baseball who helps the team finish the score – the closing pitcher, frequently called the closer (CL).[42]

But, within what limits does the closer operate? Are we really sure the closer can only operate outside the rules because he is willing to do anything to win? And, most importantly, what are those rules?[43]

New Skills of Contemporary Ethics: New Scenarios of Law & Society?

The provocative title of this chapter comes from a deeper reflection on the very notion of the term 'Closer', combined with the protagonist's way of being rather than acting: beyond all appearances, including those of the media which emphasise Harvey's charisma[44] and the legal logic of a rhetoric[45] that does not allow for a reply or an exception – the bearer of contemporaneity that, little inclined to respectful[46] dialogue,[47] demands at all costs

---

42 J. Moore, 'On the Closer Position: The Save and RP Usage', *Fangraphs,* Dec. 2003; G. Couch, 'Last Three Outs Require Mental Toughness on the Part of a Closer', *Baseball Digest*, 63 (2004).

43 For an interesting insight into *transnational litigation,* see A. Dondi, 'Legal ethics and lawyering in transnational litigation. Some scattered hints', *DPCE Online*, no. 1 (2022).

44 'So much is communicated in tone of voice, in subtleties of expression, and in body language': S. Sotomayor, *My Beloved World* (New York: Knopf, 2013).

45 To be understood, among others, also according to Habermas' theory of communicative action (G. Tieghi, 'Ripensare la Repubblica tra partecipazione e dibattito pubblico locale: "If we can keep it"', in M. Bertolissi (ed.), *Regione Veneto 1970–2020. Il futuro estratto dai fatti* (Venezia: Marsilio, 2020): from 506) also through the application of 'law as communicative experience' (G. Tieghi, 'Diritto, esperienze comunicative, Questioning: nuovi itinerari di Giustizia costituzionale'?, *Federalismi.it,* no. 14 (2020)).

46 'A respectful dialogue with one's opponent almost invariably goes further than a harangue outside his or her window. If you want to change someone's mind, you must understand what need shapes his or her opinion. To prevail, you must first listen': S. Sotmayor, *My beloved world*, quot.

47 As I was taught, there are essays that are worth rereading several times. Among them, in particular, as a guide to deontology and forensic ethics: P. Calamandrei, '*Elogio dei giudici scritto da*

from the lawyer, that the climax be directed towards the result[48] the closer of *Suits* does not, in fact, represent the unrestrained triumph of individualist logic.

On the contrary, in the complex process of approaching the result (made up of obstacles to be overcome),[49] he includes the relational dimension, the team game ('Loyalty is a two-way street. If *I* demand it from you, then you'll get it from me').

The degree of openness to the community thus to the rules that guide the community,[50] also gives substantive legal content to normative imperatives on the ethical level. In this way, almost indirectly, the so-called legal consciousness is used to explore not only the legal world, but also 'how do people obtain their knowledge of law' that is, 'how people's experiences and understanding of law are translated into action and how social action in turn constitutes their relationship to the law'.[51] But there is something else: 'If you're the smartest person in the room you're in the wrong room' (Specter). As authoritatively stated, it is imperative to be ready – to become what you want to become and to do the work you want to do – 'to be open to wanting to learn and give at the same time'.[52] First of all, a collectivity, that apparently remains in the background, that materializes, in the law firm, Pearson&Hardman (internal

---

un avvocato' (Milano: Ponte alle Grazie, 2013). For an update on the assessment of constitutional legitimacy, see, recently, M. Bertolissi, 'L'udienza pubblica dinanzi la Corte costituzionale', in M. Bertolissi, G. Bergonzini, G. Tieghi, '*Corte costituzionale in pubblico. L'autorevolezza del giudice*' (Napoli: Jovene, 2023).

48 'And after a time you may recognise that the proper measure of success is not how much you've closed the distance to some far-off goal but the quality of what you've done today': S. Sotomayor, *My beloved world*, quot.

49 Of which approximation theory is also an essential part, in G. Terranova, *Elogio dell'approssimazione. Il diritto come esperienza comunicativa* (Pisa: Pacini, 2015).

50 ' law can never be a tool for the games of power or some kind of bet on the future, but is an institutional promise that must be taken seriously by all and kept by all with every commitment': U. Vincenti, *Law and Lies*, quot.: 19. ' as you discover the strength you can draw from your community in this world from which it lives apart, look also outside of it and not only within it. Build bridges instead of walls': S. Sotomayor, *My Beloved World. From the Bronx to the Supreme Court*, quot., 233.

51 On the subject of 'Legal ideology and consciousness' as 'a third major area of law and society scholarship', see: L. Mather, *Law and Society*, in R. E. Goodin (ed.), *Handbook of Political Science* (Oxford: OUP, 2013): 8.

52 S. Sotomayor, *Lecture*, University of Stanford, 10 March 2017, at https://news.stanford.edu/2017/03/10/justice-sonia-sotomayor-speaks-stanford/#:~:text=U.S.%20Supreme%20Court%20Justice%20Sonia,which%20seats%20more%20than%201%2C700

profile), with its dynamics and its daily struggles,[53] in a representation of the legal world that struggles, often disappointingly, to create spaces for professional ethics.[54]

Secondly, a collectivity that is always at stake: this is the whole of society (external profile), a mirror of the constant search for spaces of institutional ethics, even through its TV idols, to 'educate in the cult of justice'.[55] It is Harvey himself who admonishes: 'You always have a choice'.

Specter is clearly the best, but Mike is – as Harvey himself will admit – his alter ego. The relationship that binds them will very soon go far beyond the professional bond.[56]

'It is out of law that human justice springs; and, on the other hand, it is the idea and feeling of justice present in all of us that grounds law'.[57] This, even to the point of being shown the way: 'Fight for the things that you care about, but do it in a way that will lead others to join you'.[58] Law & Society, in action.

---

53 Because 'law continues to be produced and applied unceasingly everywhere, every moment of the day and night': U. Vincenti, *Diritto e menzogna*, quot.: 18.

54 On the 'lawyers' role in our democracies' in times of crisis, and for an analysis of the 'traditional values of the legal profession,' Associate Justice N. Gorsuch spoke, in the light of his experience, at a *lecture* for Padua students during the '*Meeting the Justice*' meeting held at the University of Padua School of Law, on July 24, 2019. The advice to the Italian students was to practice law practice in a more modest-sized firm; this was precisely to grow and learn, including learning the human profile of the profession (among other things, perfectly in line with the teaching of Associate Justice S. Sotomayor in *My Beloved World*, quot: 354–355). U. Vincenti, *Diritto e menzogna*, quot., 8.

55 U. Vincenti, *Diritto e menzogna*, quot., 8.

56 'It doesn't matter! If someone comes to you and threatens you, you come to me. I don't care [...] if it's the Queen of England, you come to me! You tell me! You tell me everything! That's what [...] loyalty is!" (to Mike).

57 U. Vincenti, *Diritto e menzogna*, quot: 3.

58 A. Vagianos, *The Huffington Post features Justice Ginsburg's remarks at the Institute Radcliffe*, at https://www.radcliffe.harvard.edu/news-and-ideas/ruth-bader-ginsburg-tells-young-women-fight-for-the-things-you-care-about. Because, among other things, as Henry Ford recalled, 'getting together is a beginning, staying together is progress', but more importantly, 'working together is success'.

Chapter 9

CHARLIE HEBDO'S GRAPHIC TRIAL REPORTS (CABU, RISS, BOUCQ)

Yasco Horsman

Introduction

In 2021, Charlie Hebdo's press, Les Échappés, published *Janvier 2015, Le Procès*, a sober, well-documented book about the trial of the terrorist attacks on the journal that shook the world in 2015.[1] The trial, which took place from 2 September to 16 December 2020, brought 14 people to the dock who were accused of having been accomplices to the terrorists (who themselves had died during the attacks), and gave survivors, family, police and hostages the chance to give a testimony of the events, often for the first time. Written by Yannick Haenel and illustrated by François Boucq – who had both joined the editorial team of *Charlie Hebdo* after 2015, and first published in daily instalments on the journal's website and in weekly dispatches in the journal – the book gives a subdued but detailed depiction of the proceedings, fulfilling the request of *Charlie Hebdo*'s chief editor, Riss, to create a written monument for the victims of the attack.

Janvier 2015 is in many ways a unique work. Haenel's writing is precise and factual but its tone is mournful and engaging, and Boucq's sober illustrations in ink and watercolours beautifully evoke the atmosphere in the courtroom without being sentimental. As Cynthia Rose remarked in her review in *The Comics Journal*, the book's use of a combination of images and words to report on the trial also draws attention to a genre of graphic journalism in which the journal has been a pioneer, namely that of the graphic trial report.[2] Graphic trial reports are non-fiction comics that report on trials. It is a minor genre of

1 Y. Haenel and F. Boucq, *Janvier 2015: Le Procès* (Paris: Charlie Hebdo: Les Échappés, 2021).

2 C. Rose, 'Charlie and the Courtroom', 9 March 2021, https://www.tcj.com/charlie-and-the-courtroom/.

comics that flourished in the journal after it had come under the editorship of Philippe Val in 1992, and started to print 'serious' journalism and graphic non-fiction to accompany the editorial cartoons and humoristic pieces it is better known for.[3] *Charlie Hebdo* published a large number of such graphic trial reports, dealing with various topics, ranging from the highly politicised trials of the National Front and Scientology to trials of corrupt businessmen, murderers and petty criminals. The length of these reports varies. Some are just a page long. Other reports were published in the journal in instalments and later brought out as separate paperback booklets, as part of the *Charlie Hebdo Hors-Série* or as hard-backed books, for example Tignous and Pagnelli's *Le procès Colonna* (2015) and Riss's *Le Procès Papon: Un Fonctionnaire de Vichy au Service de la Shoah* (2017).[4]

Although drawn by different artists working in recognisably different styles, the trial reports form a remarkable coherent body of work. In fact, they share a series of distinctive features: they employ the same narrative style, use very similar types of page layout and share key stylistic choices. Their overall tone is markedly different from the often provocative and outrageous editorial cartoons the journal is better known for. The trial reports can be humorous, yet their comic sensibility is not so much 'bète et méchant', but subtle and ironical. As former editor Cavanna wrote in the preface to Riss's report on the Touvier trial, in *Charlie*'s trial reports we can recognise a 'second house style' of the journal, a collective style that differs from its 'first house style', the cartoons.[5]

This essay is an attempt to analyse this group's style. I want to spell out what is typical of Charlie's trial reports, both in terms of style, narrative mode and in comic sensibility. I will do so by zooming in on the graphic trial reports made by Cabu (Jean Cabut, 1938–2015) and Riss (Laurent Sourisseau, 1966) in the 1980s and 1990s. Cabu and Riss are pioneers of the genre. Their works introduced the conventions and style that were later adopted by artists such as Luz and Tignous, and that are still used by a younger generation that

3 For a history of the journal see C. Delporte, *Charlie Hebdo: La Folle Histoire d'un Journal Pas Comme les Autres* (Paris: Flammarion, 2020), J. Weston, '*Bête et Méchant:* Politics, Editorial Cartoons and *Bande Dessinée* in the French Satirical Newspaper *Charlie Hebdo*', *European Comic Art*, 2, no. 1 (2009): 109–129; and Y. Horsman, 'What was *Charlie Hebdo*? Blasphemy, Laughter, Politics', *Patterns of Prejudice*, 54, no. 1 (2020): 168–181.

4 Riss, *Le Procès Touvier* (Paris: Charlie Hebdo Hors-série no. 1, 1994); Riss, *Le Tour de France du Crime* (Paris: Charlie Hebdo Hors-série no. 11, 1999); Tignous and D. Pagnelli, *Le Procès Colonna* (Grenoble: Glénat, 2015); Riss, *Le Procès Papon: Un Fonctionnaire de Vichy au Service de la Shoah* (Paris: Charlie Hebdo – Les Échappés, 2015).

5 Cavanna, 'Préface' in: Riss (see note 4): 6.

currently publishes in the journal, such as Alice or Biche. In this chapter, I will specifically focus on a series of three reports, those on the cases of Klaus Barbie (by Cabu) and of Paul Touvier and Maurice Papon (both by Riss), war criminals that were tried for having committed crimes against humanity in 1987, 1994 and 1998. Each of these trials drew an unprecedented amount of media attention. I will argue that Cabu's and Riss's reports implicitly respond to this media attention as well, thereby reflecting on the role of the trial in the public sphere.

Cabu on the Trial of Klaus Barbie

A good starting point for studying the emergence of the *Charlie* style of reporting on trials can be found in a short 12-page comic drawn by Cabu, entitled 'La fin des Aventures de Barbie Fridolin' (The End of Barbie Kraut's Adventures), which was not published *in Charlie Hebdo* but in its competitor *Le Canard Enchainé*, in the period after the journal had ceased publication in 1981 and before it was resurrected in 1992.[6] Cabu had been one of the star artists of the journal's first team of cartoonists. He was famous for his biting editorial cartoons as well as for his pioneering work in graphic journalism. He had published travelogues, reportages on political manifestations and graphic reports of trips into the provinces of France. The comic published in *Le Canard* seems, at first sight, a minor entry in Cabu's rich body of work. The comic seems to be drawn rather quickly. Its interest for us lies in the first place in its subject matter, the trial of Klaus Barbie which took place in Lyon in 1987, and which had attracted massive attention from the broadcast media and the printing press. As Alice Kaplan explains in an essay that looks back at the trial, this media attention was not something that was *external* to the trial.[7] To those involved, it was deemed to be an essential feature. Filmed in its entirety (but not to be released until 20 years after the trial), the trial was widely regarded as being of historic significance, a moment when the nation faced its past. Watching the proceedings was thought to have a didactic impact, especially on the nation's youth. During the trial, schoolchildren were regularly brought into the courtroom to watch the proceedings, and didactic material was made available to teachers so that the case could be discussed in classrooms. Like the Eichmann trial, which had taken place 27 years earlier, the

6 Cabu, 'La Fin des Aventures de Barbie Fridolin' (1987), reprinted in *Tenoua Hors-Série: La Justice après le Shoah* (Paris, 2018): 50–61.

7 A. Kaplan, 'On Alain Finkielkraut's "Remembering in Vain" The Klaus Barbie Trial and Crimes Against Humanity', *Critical Inquiry*, 19, no. 1 (1992): 70–86.

Barbie trial was widely believed to be more than just a trial. It was spoken of as a quasi-therapeutic moment in which the nation could come to terms with its past.[8]

With its 12 pages, 'Barbie Fridolin' is a rather modest contribution to the large body of literature on the Barbie case. Stylistically, it is a rather uneven work. Its first six pages provide a sketchy narrative of the trial, while the second half consists largely of a series of editorial cartoons that depict Barbie in various absurd situations: hanging on a butcher's meat hook (in an allusion to his nickname 'the butcher of Lyon'), lying sideways on the floor as a pig who is happily sucking a group of five newborn fascist piglets or having a fancy dinner with his prison guards, complaining about the wine ('No! No Bordeaux with oysters. It is a crime against humanity!') As is typical of Cabu's editorial cartoons, the mode of these drawings is opinionated and slightly provocative. They seek to provide a commentary on Barbie, a judgement even.

These drawings are preceded by a series of pages that contain images that are markedly different, both in tone and style. The cartoons are drawn by a steady hand that uses heavy black outlines. The images in the first part of the comic are drawn with much thinner lines. They seem improvised, sketchy, unfinished. They do not so much focus on the figure of Barbie but they evoke the setting of the trial, the city of Lyon and the courtroom in which the proceedings took place. More importantly, the mood of these drawings differs from the cartoon-like drawings. They are observational, not judgemental. They are drawn from the perspective of someone who is present in the courtroom and watches the proceedings unfold with a pencil in his hand and sketchbook on his lap.

These sketchy pages also draw attention to a key aspect of the Barbie trial, the omnipresence of the media. In his sketches of the scenes in and around the courtroom, Cabu shows cameras, microphones, notebooks and representatives of the 650 journalists who had come to Lyon to report on the trial. The comic evokes the buzzing sense of anticipation that is present among the journalists and police officers as they await the arrival of the accused. And it shows how they are starstruck when Barbie finally appears. 'It is a bit like Cannes,' Cabu writes, 'with cops who barely conceal their desire to ask for an autograph'. Cabu is initially bemused by this excitement. He describes ironically the inevitable feeling of disappointment that sets in once the trial has started ('I should have gone to Cannes,' a journalist sighs). But he ends his

8 For an overview of the discussion about the didactic and therapeutic function of the Eichmann trial, see: Y. Horsman, *Theatres of Justice: Judging, Staging and Working Through in Arendt, Brecht and Delbo* (Stanford: Stanford University Press, 2010).

report with a biting cartoon in which he raises the question of whether the media's fascination with Barbie had not undermined the goals of the trial. This cartoon depicts Barbie after the trial, seated in his cell in a comfortable chair, accompanied by two relaxing prison guards, watching a television broadcast of Claude Lanzmann's *Shoah*. Seemingly content with himself, he smiles at the prison guards and exclaims, 'Just wait when the footage of my trial will be released! My film will be as big as *Shoah*. I will surely win a Cesar!'

In his comic, Cabu points to a tension at the heart of the Barbie trial. On the one hand, its publicity was an inextricable part of the trial. Since the trial hoped to convey 'lessons' about the past to a larger audience, it had to be brought into the public sphere. Yet, as Cabu suggests, the media's obsessive interest in the trial undermined the lessons it hoped to teach. By putting him in the spotlight, the media had turned Barbie into a star. The filming of the trial, which sought to deflate the figure of Barbie, only triggered a fascination with the old Nazi, Cabu seems to hold.

In his critique of the trial, Cabu makes a point that was also made by philosopher Alan Finkielkraut, who, like Cabu, had come to Lyon to report on the proceedings. In the postface to the book he wrote on the trial, *Remembering in Vain*, Finkielkraut is highly sceptical of the media attention the trial received.[9] The media, Finkielkraut holds, have a logic of their own. Broadcasting images from a trial is therefore not without risks. It involves taking the trial into a sphere in which a different dynamic prevails than in the courtroom. It means subjecting the trial to the one law that rules supreme in the media, that is the law of entertainment. Broadcasting a trial on television therefore undermines its didactic and pedagogical goals. Finkielkraut writes:

> The confidence in the pedagogical and therapeutic virtues of the television screen is based on a postulate: that television is a neutral instrument, a simple means of communication that has no effect on the subject matter it transmits. (70)

This is, however, not the case, Finkielkraut states. There is a profound difference between watching a trial in the courtroom and watching images of a trial on television, in the privacy of our homes, where we can be distracted by the worries of our everyday lives. A trial needs to take place in a setting that is radically separated from the mundanity of the everyday. The exclamation 'Court is in Session!' that announces the beginning of legal proceedings

9 A. Finkielkraut, *Remembering in Vain: The Klaus Barbie Trial and Crimes against Humanity* (New York: Columbia University Press, 1992).

serves to create a distinction between the legal sphere and that of the everyday. Finkielkraut writes:

> 'Court is in Session!': bodily functions have to be brought under control, the drone of daily life has to be suspended so that the judicial ceremony can unfold. (70)

The same goes for teaching, religious ceremonies and the theatre. They can only take place in spaces that are separated from the everyday.

> The same principle holds true, in fact, for justice as for religion, for theatre or for the act of teaching – it can be done anywhere (a table suffices) but only by isolating the time and space of these interactions from their secular settings. (70)

The media then – and film and television in particular – do indeed bring the trial to the public. But in doing so, they profoundly change its nature, Finkielkraut concludes. And that is a bad thing, he holds.

Cabu seems to be similarly suspicious of the presence of cameras in the courtroom. This is at least indicated by the opening page of the comic, which depicts the courtroom as an enclosed space that is penetrated by two cameras: a security camera in the upper right corner of the page (which is compared to an observation tower) and the cameras of a television crew in the lower right corner. Both cameras seem to *open* the enclosed space of the courtroom and to give entry to the sensationalistic gaze of starstruck journalists, who dream of Cannes and of collecting autographs.

In his comic, then, Cabu opposes two different spaces, that of the courtroom and that of the media, as well as two different gazes, a legal and a journalistic one. Each one looks at the trial with a different attitude and pays attention to different aspects of the trial. Implicit in the comic, however, is a *third* gaze, that of Cabu himself, whose improvised sketches evoke the experience of being present *in* the courtroom while listening with the fleeting attention of someone who is neither a journalist nor a judge or a lawyer, but a sketch artist, who listens as he draws and whose fleeting attention tunes in to different aspects of the trial, without giving in to the sensationalism of the media. 'La fin des Aventures de Barbie Fridolin' then offers only a critique of the media – it also provides for an alternative way of reporting on the trial.

Riss on the Trials of Papon and Touvier

In the space of a few pages, Cabu's comic delivers a critique of the way in which the Barbie trial was treated in the media, and he explores new ways of reporting on the trial that do not give in to the pitfalls of sensationalism.

In his sketches of the courtroom, he furthermore introduces a drawing style that would become characteristic of the trial reports that *Charlie Hebdo* would publish in the 1990s, after the journal had restarted in 1992. This new *Charlie*, now under the editorship of Philippe Val, brought together the cartoonists who had published in the older *Charlie* (Wolinski, Cabu, Willem, Gébé) with a new generation of artists (Charb, Riss, Luz, Tignous) who produced editorial cartoons that were very much in the spirit of *Charlie* – provocative, outrageous, sometimes blasphemous. The journal now combined these editorial cartoons with pieces of written investigative journalism, and various forms of graphic non-fiction, such as travelogues, reportages, diary-like pieces, and indeed, trial reports, drawn by the same artists who also made editorial cartoons (Tignous, Cabu, Luz or later Alice and Biche).

The most prolific author of such trial reports was Riss. Throughout the 1990s, Riss published hundreds of pages of graphic trial reports in the journal. Some of them were just a few pages long and reported on small crimes. Other reports were substantially longer, such as the reports on the trials of war criminals Paul Touvier and Maurice Papon, which run well into the hundreds of pages and were reprinted as separate books.

In these works, Riss developed a particular style of reporting, the most characteristic feature of which is that he limits himself to depicting *exclusively* that which is visible within the confines of the courtroom. This decision is announced on the opening pages of Riss's trial reports, which typically contain large double-paged depictions of the stage on which the legal drama unfolds, the courtrooms of Bordeaux (in the Papon case), or that of Paris (in Touvier's case), which are peopled by judges, defence lawyers, prosecutors, members of the jury and, in both cases, the accused (Barbie and Papon) who sit behind a screen of protective glass. Riss's shorter trial reports, collected in the book *Tour de France de Crime* (1999), open with similar detailed depictions of courtrooms in Amiens, Caen, Nimes, Orleans and other places. In these images, he draws attention to the law's mundane administrative accoutrements: the dossiers, notebooks and lawbooks, as well as the technology necessary for the proceedings (microphones, amplifiers, lights). But he also zooms in on the imposing architecture of the buildings in which the trial takes place. Often depicted from low angles that show decorated ceilings, busts, sets of columns or artworks that depict the iconography of the law (justitia, in the heavens, surrounded by angels), these drawings evoke large spaces in which the protagonists of the trial appear diminished and small. These monumental, often windowless rooms show a world that is separated from the everyday and that seems to enclose the participants, closing them off from the world.

Riss's trial reports never leave these spaces. He strictly limits himself to depicting the drama that takes place within the walls of the courtroom, drawing large pages filled with talking figures and large chunks of dialogue that are rendered verbatim. These figures are introduced by tiny captions that mention dates and names but rarely provide more information. Riss's trial reports typically do not include a *voice-over* that reflects on the meaning of the trial. He gives no commentary or draws conclusions. Nor do the reports include flashbacks or visualizations of crimes. He sticks exclusively to that which is visible inside the courtroom.

Like Cabu, Riss uses black and white line drawings, whose level of detail changes throughout his trial reports. At times, his images are elaborate and detailed, with many cross-hatches; at other times they have been drawn quickly and roughly, sketched in just a few lines. By leaving in unfinished elements or mistakes, the drawings seem improvised. They point our attention to the act of drawing itself and, by extension, to the artist who is present at the proceedings. As a result, the drawings do not only provide a representation of the trial, but they also evoke the presence of a person watching the events unfold with the specific mode of attentiveness of someone who is listening as he draws – sometimes focused, sometimes drifting off, sometimes side-tracked by insignificant details.

Riss's reports, then, testify to the *experience* of being present at the trial. His drawings can be seen as examples of what Hilary Chute calls an act of *graphic witnessing*, visual testimonies of first-hand experiences.[10] The book's fluctuations in style, its varying levels of detail – ranging from elaborated to quickly sketched – and its changes in tone (from sober to caricatural) conjure up, indirectly, the feeling of being stuck in a courtroom, when one's boredom, ennui and stagnation (indicated by doodling and extensive cross-hatching) are interrupted by moments when something interesting or funny happens, which is sketched in faster, livelier lines.

These moments of comic relief are typically provided by the behaviour of the accused and their lawyers. Or to be more precise, the comedy in the courtroom, as drawn by Riss, is provided by the *gestures* of his protagonists: the pompous gesticulations that accompany professions of innocence, or the feigned indignation at certain accusations. During the Touvier case, it is the lawyer, Maître Trémolet de Villers, who provokes Riss's mirth, as he depicts him as a grotesque figure whose melodramatic body language recalls the lawyers depicted by Daumier. During a trial in Orleans, it is the accused who preposterously flaunts his innocence in a series of wild gesticulations, drawn in a fast kinetic style that provokes laughter. And in the Papon case, Riss's

10 H. Chute, *Disaster Drawn. Visual Witness, Comics and Documentary Form* (Cambridge: Harvard University Press, 2016).

most elaborate trial report, it is the former Vichy official himself who seems to be adopting a series of postures that seem borrowed from rhetorical handbooks and old-fashioned actors' guides, expressing his disbelief, anger and impatience as he listens to the proceedings, while similarly desperately trying to project a certain respectability.[11]

By citing these gestures and condensing them into a series of poses, Riss manages to distil what Bertolt Brecht calls the *gestus* of his characters, the gesture that exhibits in concentrated form an attitude that is typical of a social group.[12] Riss's images, however, depict not so much the class background of his characters (as Brecht tried to do) but the *attitude* that they adopt in the courtroom and the *masks* they wear to conceal their guilt. These drawings are comical. But their comic sensibility is different from that of the caricaturist. As Jane Weston points out in her study of the journal, *Charlie Hebdo's* caricatures were typically aimed at a specific target: hypocrisy.[13] In its cartoons, the journal sought to *unmask* politicians, revealing the pathological, gluttonous, or sexually perverse bodies that hide behind the seemingly respectable mask of authority, and the corruption of individuals that stains the dignity of the offices that they hold. Riss's trial reports, on the other hand, focus their attention on the *persona* that people adopt in the courtroom, the *masks* that they wear on the legal stage. He shows, for example, how Maurice Papon, the former Vichy functionary, lets himself be addressed as *monsieur le ministre* by his defence lawyer, in an attempt to reclaim some of the dignity of his former role. By desperately clinging to the status this former role provided, Riss shows, Papon could remain blind to the consequences of his acts.

This becomes clear when we turn to a double-page spread included towards the end of *Le procès Papon* entitled, 'Papon: il nous enterrera tous' (Papon, he will bury us all). The spread depicts 15 similarly sized Papon-figures, gesticulating and responding to the testimonies of the victims. The pages form a montage of several different moments in which Papon seeks to exculpate himself using a string of theatrical gestures and empty phrases, flaunting his indignation at the accusations ('What would you have done in my place? What about the Germans?'), using pretentious words ('it's all logomachy!'), expressing impatience ('have I now satisfied your curiosity?'), being overly

11 For a more detailed study of *Le Procès Papon,* see *Yasco Horsman*, 'Laughter in the Courts of Law: On Riss's Graphic Report on the Papon Trial', *Law, Culture and the Humanities*, 7 February 2023, https://journals.sagepub.com/doi/full/10.1177/17438721221116554

12 B. Brecht, 'A Short Organum for the Theatre,' [1949] *Brecht on Theatre: The Development of an Aesthetic,* ed. and transl. John Willett (London: Methuen, 1964), 170-205

13 J. Weston, 'Charlie Hebdo and Joyful Resistance', in *European Connections*, ed. Peter Collier (Bern: Peter Lang, 2006): 201–246, 236.

pious ('those poor people who were sent away') or addressing the prosecution as 'men of honour', while standing up, adjusting his belt and his tie. 'Despite the facts that overwhelmed him', Riss adds in a rare aside, 'the old crocodile didn't doubt about his innocence, and definitely not about himself'.

This sequence shows the narcissistic pleasure Papon finds in assuming the role of a dignitary, in playing *monsieur le ministre* in public. Furthermore, the precise location of these pages – at the heart of the section of victims' testimonies – intimates that a similar type of narcissism, which now causes him to remain deaf to the suffering of the victims during the trial, may have enabled him to perform his duties as a functionary during the period under examination in the proceedings.

Conclusion

Central to Charlie Hebdo's graphic trial reports, as developed in the pioneering work of Riss and Cabu, is a decision to report from *inside* the spaces of the courtroom. By focusing exclusively on the proceedings that took place during the trial, and by zooming in on the words and *gestures* of the figures on the legal stage, these reports do justice to the fact that a trial, as Alain Finkielkraut argues, takes place in a sphere that is isolated from the mundanity of everyday life. The reports, then, seek to maintain the separation of the sphere of law from the everyday that, according to Finkielkraut, is introduced by the call, 'Court is in session!'

In their attempt to preserve the distinction between the trial and the everyday, Charlie's trial reports are surprisingly close to the older, perhaps more conservative tradition of the journalistic courtroom sketches that appear in newspapers. As art historian Lynda Nead explains, courtroom sketches first appeared in the media after photography was banned from the courtrooms. This ban, she explains, was introduced not only to protect the privacy of the people involved in a trial but also to preserve the dignity of the trial, which was felt to be threatened when newspaper journalists entered the courtroom.[14] As Nead writes, 'the newspapers brought the public into the courtroom; they penetrated its enclosed and rarified space', (63) thereby undermining the trial as 'a discrete and pure space for the exercise of justice'. (63) Banning photography served to keep the journalistic gaze out of the courtroom. Nead writes:

14 L. Nead, 'Freedom from Publicity or Right to Information? Visual Cultures of the Courtroom', in *Legal Stagings. The Visualization, Medialization and Ritualization of Law in Language, Literature, Media, Art and Architecture*, ed. K. Modéer and M. Sunnqvist (Copenhagen: University of Copenhagen Press, 2012): 60–83.

> It was the power of the photograph 'to be there' in the court [...] that worried the legislators [...] The prohibition of photography effectively removed the mass public from the courtroom and prevented the law being turned into an emotive spectacle. (81)

The courtroom sketch that developed after the ban of photography was a compromise, Nead explains. It did give the public access to the legal process, which was necessary since justice must be *seen* to be done. But it adds distance as well. The characteristic hand-drawn style of the courtroom sketch, which makes us aware of 'the artifice and agency of the artist',[15] foregrounds the fact that it does not give us *direct* access to the courtroom. "The courtroom sketch,' Nead concludes, 'does not infiltrate the hermetically sealed world of the courtroom as the camera would do but maintains and strengthens the essential borderline between the inside and the outside of the legal process'. (80)

Riss's drawings similarly respect the borderline that separates the sphere of law from that of everyday life. He refuses to cross this border, stays in the courtroom and zooms in on the gestures, body language and postures of the figures that act on the legal stage, depicting the attitudes that these figures protagonists adopt and the masks that they put on to hide their guilt.

Surprisingly, masks also turned out to play a key role in the illustrations Boucq made for *Janvier 2015*. As the trial of the terrorist attacks on Charlie Hebdo took place during the corona crisis, everyone in the courtroom wore face masks. In an interview given after the publication of the book, Boucq admits that this frustrated him at first. He had hoped to see faces and draw portraits. But he discovered soon that the masks forced him to direct his attention to something far more revealing: the body language of the people in the dock. 'What underlines someone's interiority is the way he holds his hands', he explains, 'how he approaches the bar, how he moves his feet'.[16]

Sketching bodies, rather than faces, enabled him to see something in the courtroom that had escaped the attention of the other participants, a posture that betrays an attitude that perhaps can only be captured by a sketch artist who is not blinded by a fascination with individual criminals, but who watches their movements with the detached and relaxed gaze of someone who holds a pencil, a piece of paper and a set of watercolours.

---

15 L. Nead, 'Courtroom Sketching: Reflections on History, Law and the Image', in *Law and Popular Culture*, ed. M. Freeman (Oxford: Oxford University Press, 2005): 182.

16 Boucq, cited in Rose (see note 3).

Chapter 10

EPILOGUE

Giuseppe Martinico and Gianpaolo Maria Ruotolo

I'll give you justice, I'll fathom your purse
Show me your moral that you reversed
I hear me holler, I hear me moan
I pay in blood but not my own

(Bob Dylan, *I pay in blood*, 2012)

Stranger Things, the popular Netflix series, has contributed to the rediscovery of the legendary 1980s,[1] with music, stories, games and characters.

For those of us who grew up in the 1980s, many of the themes and characters explored in the previous pages are a part of our youth. Many years later, we are pleased to revisit them in a scholarly work that holds a very special meaning for us.

For us, this, to say it in Carcass' words, is a heartwork ('Food for thought, so prolific').

This, together with the good fortune of coordinating a group of extraordinary Authors, made this volume a truly unforgettable experience.

The cultural representations of law in culture, as we tried to show, are innumerable and diverse. They range from those written, thought and enjoyed by professionals, such as textbooks, commentaries and decisions, to those that tell us about law in the most diverse cultural fields, such as comics, cinema, literature, music and so on.

The group of scholars we had the honour of coordinating showed *how* the media they studied consider a representation of law that is somehow *oriented*, that is to say, they reconstruct the legal phenomenon or some of its factual elements with the aim of highlighting only some of its aspects, be they positive or negative, in order to tell us *a* story (and not *the* story) of law.

---

1 J. Vogel, *Stranger Things and the '80s: The Complete Retro Guide* (London: Cardinal Books, 2018).

Moreover, for us, these pages represent another brick in an ongoing wall built by a research agenda that we find highly promising.

This agenda builds on a strong foundation of deep relationships, some of which became friendships, and a series of prior achievements. It aims to further develop through collaboration and exploration.

We are firmly convinced, indeed, that the pages of this book can serve not only as a basis for more reflections on the connections between law and justice, as well as between law, justice and pop music in general, and graphic literature in particular. At the same time, they also serve as tools to disseminate knowledge about all these remarkable expressions of human creativity. Another aspect that emerged during these studies—and one that confirms something we deeply believe as legal scholars—is the connection between high-quality artistic expressions and law through the element of beauty. Law, and even scholarly dissertations on law, can sometimes partake in the phenomenon of beauty as creations of the human mind. Additionally, the studies hereby gathered offer an opportunity to teach comparative and international law in a less conventional, yet equally rigorous, manner.

The use of popular media, indeed, can help to describe some phenomena regulated by law and make them understandable to those who do not (still) have specific competences, thus contributing to the diffusion of legal concepts, whether from a didactic or a more informative perspective. Students will certainly be aided in their understanding of legal dynamics by the use of comics and music they know and love, which may help reduce the gap in knowledge between professors and students.

Moreover, since the artistic expressions we dealt with deeply touched human beings, they can certainly represent an incentive to reflect on the issues they face and, therefore, raise the listener's awareness of them.

***

Finally, we extend our heartfelt thanks to all the scholars, colleagues, and friends we met along the long and dusty road that brought us here—only a small part of which is published in these pages (but you know who you are!). We are also deeply grateful to our students, PhD candidates, and collaborators for being a constant source of inspiration and intellectual challenge. Many thanks to our publisher, Anthem Press, and the wonderful teams in London and New York for their invaluable support—you rule! A special mention goes to Michele Quatraro, PhD student at the University of Genoa, for his invaluable help in compiling the index. We paid in blood, but not our own.

Last but not least, we'd love to thank our academic institutions, the Scuola Superiore Sant'Anna in Pisa and the University of Foggia School of Law, for their constant support.

INDEX

Acrassiscauda 90
Allen, Tony 78
Allred, Mike 71
Anthrax 81
antidiscrimination laws 15
Antigone 7, 18
anti-personnel mines 86
Arka'n Asrafokor 94

Batman 1, 8, 19–24, 30, 48, 49
black metal music 88
Black Panther (T'Challa) 33
Bretton Woods Institutions 74

Captain America 31–33, 51
Charlie Hebdo 4, 129–31, 135, 137–39
Christmas Truce 84
Churchill, Winston 82
Consorzio Suonatori Indipendenti 79
constitution 22–23, 28
corruption 11, 19, 92, 94, 100, 103, 111, 137
crime 2, 3, 8, 65
Crimean War 83

Daredevil 1, 3, 7–16
Darkthrone 89
DC 3, 33
Dent (Two-Face) 20
disability 10, 12–15
discrimination 3, 12, 18–19, 24, 27, 30–32, 34, 38, 40, 50
Dylan, Bob 78–79

Enslaved 89
Exodus 88

Felton Outcault, Richard 70
Filemón 100–13
Franco, Francisco (Caudillo) 99, 109
fundamental rights (human rights) 73, 77–78, 82–84, 88, 90–92

Gordon James (Jim) (Commissioner Gordon) 19–21, 49
Gotham 19–21, 23
graphic journalism 4, 129, 131

Harry Potter 54–55, 57–58, 60–64
heavy metal music 90

Ibáñez Talavera, Francisco 4, 97
identity politics 26–28, 41, 45–47, 49, 51–52
inclusion 12–13, 16, 32, 46
International Confederation of Wizards (ICW) 54–55, 58, 60
international humanitarian law 27, 84–85
international law 1, 3, 53, 56–57, 59, 64, 67–69, 71–87, 91–92, 94–95, 142
International Statute For Magical Secrecy 54
invisibility 12
Iron Maiden 82

Joe Chill 21
Joker 20–21, 49
Judas Priest 81
Judge Dredd 81
justice 1, 2, 6–11, 14, 17–22, 24, 31, 33, 36, 38, 49, 94, 112, 120, 124, 128, 134, 138, 139, 142

Kent, Clark 22
Kirby, Jack 32, 70
Kuti, Fela 73, 78
Kuti, Seun 74

Law and Literature 2
legal culture 115–20
legal drama 4, 115–16, 119, 121, 135

magic 56, 58, 62–63
Magneto 25–26, 34–37, 45, 48
Manga 2, 7, 30, 71
Marvel 3, 7, 12, 24–25, 32–33, 38, 47–49, 52, 70–71
Megadeth 86–87
Metal Hurlant/Heavy Metal 71
Metallica 85
morality 1, 3, 19
Mortadelo 100–13
Muddy Waters 70
Murder Falcon 70–71
Murdock, Matthew 3, 7–8, 10–12, 15

natural law 22

Orphaned Land 89, 123

Phoenix 38, 55, 61
police 19–20, 22–23, 37, 44–45, 129, 132
pop culture, pop legal culture 1, 2, 17, 31, 115–19, 125, 142
Profesor Bacterio 106–8, 110–11
Professor X (Xavier, Charles Francis) 35–36
public ethics 115

racial equality 33
Reaper (Caspian, Judson) 21
recognition 12, 14, 26, 33–36, 46, 94, 102, 112
Refugee All-Stars of Sierra Leone 76
refugees 76, 80
religion 3, 19, 35, 41, 43, 76, 87–88, 134
revenge 2, 9, 21, 47, 49, 107
Rowling, Joanne K. 53–55, 57–59, 64

Sabaton 83–84
Sarajevo 79
Security Council (UN) 55, 74, 78, 87
self-determination 16, 46, 58–59, 64, 75, 83

www.ingramcontent.com/pod-product-compliance
Ingram Content Group UK Ltd.
Pitfield, Milton Keynes, MK11 3LW, UK
UKHW041831100926
8556IPUK00002B/122

9 781839 993664